'A style of unshowy distinction, and penetrating insights into female psychology, make Pauline Neville's *The Cousins*, set just before and during the second world war, a highly readable novel ... Neville has provided a moving evocation of her chosen period' – Francis King, *Sunday Telegraph*

'A marvellous novel which pierces both the heart and mind with its sad wisdom and flashes of gay wonder' – Kay Dick, *The Scotsman*

'There is remarkable courage in this writer ... a little gem of personal revelation' – *Country Life*

'Her writing is subtle, absorbing, complex and often brilliant' – *Sydney Morning Herald*

Pauline Neville

PEGGY

ARCADIA BOOKS
LONDON

Arcadia Books Ltd
15–16 Nassau Street
London WIN 7RE

First published in Great Britain 1999
© Pauline Neville 1999

A catalogue record for this book is available
from the British Library.

ISBN 1–900850–17–6

Typeset in Monotype Fournier by Discript, London WC2N 4BL
Printed in Finland by WSOY

Arcadia Books distributors are as follows:
in the UK and elsewhere in Europe:
Turnaround Publishers Services
Unit 3, Olympia Trading Estate
Coburg Road
London N22 6TZ

in the USA and Canada:
by Dufour Editions, Inc.
PO Box 7
Chester Springs, PA 19425-0007

in Australia:
Tower Books
PO Box 213
Brookvale, NSW 2100

in New Zealand:
Addenda
Box 78224
Grey Lynn
Auckland

For John

EARLY THIS MORNING, Peggy, when I was reaching up out of sleep, the screech of seagulls coming out of the storm and up the Thames estuary brought in sounds and sights of our childhood and I was back in our upright car bouncing our way off the passenger ferry from Stranraer onto the quay at Larne, the car squelching through seagull droppings and we listening to the distinctive and evocative sound of the Irish voice.

The journey south through the patchwork countryside of Northern Ireland took us on narrow roads, avoiding Belfast because signs DETOUR: FIGHTING IN THE STREETS, kept us from the centre – my English mother protesting: 'It's the Troubles again, James', and Father answering: 'But look towards the granite sweep of the Mountains of Mourne'.

Do you remember, Peggy, that from the back of our house at Ballymartin we could walk up Honeysuckle Lane on our mountain feet to the waters of the Silent Valley and look back on the sparkling sea we'd just crossed?

The names alone can do it for you, as can the notice on the side of the road as you approach Kilkeel: 'Welcome to the Kingdom of Mourne'. It's not to be forgotten that the Irish had kings long before the English were sitting on their throne. But this was not then the land of terrorists, where people were blown up in their beds, this was the quiet countryside, a chessboard of little fields, stone walls where damp moss clung, whitewashed cottages in which farmers eked out a living from one day to the next, and where the colour green dominated.

There may have been a terrorist or two skulking around, but the police knew who they were, and if the IRA had a message to get to their counterparts in the south, there would be no communication by wireless. They would write it on a piece of paper, stuff it in the toe of their sock and walk it there.

What went wrong? Inequality, the build-up of anger, and then interference from outside.

Mid-morning would see us on the mountain roads with our backs to the sea – but then we'd have been in it earlier when shafts of sunlight were making golden saucers on the water, and the herring fisher-men coming in with their catch, their sea-battered boats covered in salt spray and seagull droppings.

But you are saying: 'I don't think it was white and grey Mary wore every day at Ballymartin. That was for Sundays.'

'Oh good, Peggy, you are *remembering*.'

Mary's grey hair was tied back with pins, pieces straggling over her face and some falling into the soup or the baking of the soda bread.

'D'you remember that on the day Mary baked, the kitchen was out of bounds to the family?'

'Never mind that wandering dogs, cats and a goat or two would come through the back door.'

Puffs of wheaten flour would appear from under

the shut door and soon the house would be full of the sharp rising of the soda bread.

Mary was old. She'd always been without teeth, Father said. I never saw her in anything but a pale blue maid's dress and large white apron. She slept in the boiler-room, I'm ashamed to say; any maid we brought over from Scotland had to sleep in there with her.

She was, of course, Protestant. We never employed those who were Roman Catholic, mainly I think because Father, who, amongst other aspects of his multifarious personality, was a Presbyterian minister, could not countenance the sight of a bleeding Christ on the Cross, whether hanging round necks or on the walls. The point about Christianity, he said, was the *risen* Christ.

'She's of the Faith.'

'Who Peggy?'

'Nuala.' You look towards the Irish nurse just coming into the room. You scowl through your smile. Might there be a bit of a fight in there for you? But this time Nuala pats you on the head, nods towards me, smiles, is gone again, and you are asleep.

Our journey from Galloway in south-west Scotland took place in the middle of the night. The boat for Northern Ireland left at dawn and we had to come on slow twisting roads in a car where the top register was 35. Inside the car is Father (your Uncle James), Mother (your Aunt Marj), brother Mike, our maid Annie, our dog, Oats, and myself. We in the back sat on bundles of towels, swimming costumes, buckets, spades, cricket bat, balls, and a large bottle of iodine.

Oats had the greatest feeling for Ireland of us all, because it was only as he stepped off the boat onto Irish soil that he allowed his imprint, flowing freely, onto the quay. Annie was always sick going up the gangplank because she'd been told about seasickness and thought it best to get it over early on. One year we took Moffat the cat, hoping that if we kept an eye on her sexual rampagings we would avoid the litters waiting for us on our return.

Our annual visit to our Irish grandmother re-established Father's stake on the land of his birth, and coincided with your family's summer holiday, you all waiting to greet us off the boat at Larne. We followed you down the road going south, and as we approached the Kingdom of Mourne the singing started: '*For all we could find there we might as well be/Where the Mountains of Mourne sweep down to the sea.*'

Your mother and my father were, in looks, like twins; the seven brothers and their one sister had florid faces, fathom-deep blue-grey eyes, slightly hanging jowls – Aunt Netta and Father resembling Queen Victoria in middle years – and electric smiles.

My very early memories of our Irish grandmother – because remember she died when I was young – was of size and strength and a dry humour that was under layers both of black clothes and of shrewd perception. In the summer month of August – which was our visiting time – she sat in her green canvas chair in the shady part of the garden, the hood of the chair supporting little bobbles flicking shadows over her face as the sea breezes sharpened up the garden. Members of the family came one by one to pay court to her, and she in turn would know exactly which was the offspring of which of her eight children. Her youngest son, James, destined to 'go into the Church', had married an English woman, and that took some time to get over.

In the middle of the gravel that led to the house at Ballymartin was a jagged and hideous old monkey-puzzle – worse than most – as if rats had been gnawing it since plantation occurred, and as if to go with its frenzied ugliness, Grandmother's parrot screeched at any stray dog or cat in a language learnt when adorning the captain's cabin in one of the family boats. From the parrot came a smell of tar, salt water and ocean fish, and I believe if we had taken it inland to live it would have smelt the same. We all joined in a loving hatred of this parrot and its inner certainty.

I think Grandmother was always in black, long-skirted, with hair piled on top, usually arranged by whichever poor female relation was doing service at the time.

I don't have many shared memories with you about Grandmother, because your mother, as the only girl, was the much-wanted daughter after seven boys. She was the spoilt favourite, and some of it washed off on you, and you were allowed to call her Grannie.

You move in your bed, and 'Grannie' you say.

Grandmother did not have to tell anyone to do anything twice. She spoke in imperatives and, had she been there, would have been a heroine in up-country Kenya during the time of the Mau Mau, sitting in evening dress, rigid at the head of the dining-table, the gun in her evening bag, the bag facing the door.

'Marjorie,' she said once to Mother when I was above five, 'cut that girl's hair and show the only good feature she has got.'

The hair was cut all right, and I've gone around exposing my forehead ever since.

I'm sorry never to have known either of my grandfathers. My English one, Kingsford Pawling, was a director of the famous Mudies Library, himself a cousin of the Mudies, and when the firm went bust from maintaining too high a standard it was he who had to make the workers redundant – although it's unlikely he would have known what the word meant – his heart breaking for them, and for himself a few months later. Our Irish grandfather was of sterner material. When his eldest son, Frank, was getting married, his youngest son, my father James – who was twenty-two years younger – was bought a velvet suit to honour the occasion, and when he wet the trousers from excitement, he was sent to bed and was not allowed to go to the wedding. When our grand-father died, Grandmother, for a time, took on most of his attitudes about the upbringing of a large family and ruled the household with hardly a break in continuity.

But it was your mother who stood up to Grandmother Fisher, and this may have been the root of your 'No. I won't', to this day. The nurses in here are amused by it, and are running at your beck and call. Small people, Peggy, seem to have condensed energy, and with it a powerful will.

My mother's origins, if you remember, were also Cornwall, but it was a long way from the Kensington drawing-room in which she was brought up.

Grannie Pawling came only once to Ulster. She was considered too grand for Ballymartin, County Down. I have only one memory of her in Ireland: sitting beside the Black Rock in a chair brought down to the shore for her, complete in fur tippet, looking out to sea, and wishing herself hence. Shores, sand in your clothes, popping seaweed, screaming gulls, were not for her. She preferred life as *she* saw it: streets with theatres in them, concert halls where professional musicians played, doormen who took off their hats to her, and sitting in Kensington drawing-rooms, flicking cultural references towards her bright, bright cousins, the Mudies. From the beginning of Father's courtship of Mother, inside a hospital in London during World War II, Grandmother Pawling was of the opinion that 'one did not marry the Irish', particularly not an Irish clergyman. When she came to stay in Scotland – a month at a time in those days – she wore her topcoat and hat to walk through the hall. The Scottish weather, the Scottish people, she considered to be one down from Ireland, and the Irish. North and

South of Ireland were all the same to her, all part of
the plot to do down the English. Grannie Pawling
hugged her prejudices inside her wraparound coat,
but later, we must remember, she paid for Mike's
and my public schooling. Partly, I suppose, because
she could not stand the sound of our broad Scots
accents, or the sight of unruly hair as we ran wild
with the village children.

Cultural Italy she adored, and went with the
Mudies, coach and six, across Europe, landing in a
rented palazzo on the Grand Canal in Venice. The
Mudies' addiction to cultural Italy was such that,
once back home in London, they shouted all over
the house for their Cockney male servant, Charles,
by calling out: 'Carlos, come here', and 'Carlos go
there'.

We had to drive twelve miles back and forth
every day to pick up Grannie Pawling from her hotel
in County Down, the car with its fur-lined foot muff
(given by her) and rug (given by her) the best aspect
of Ballymartin, she considered.

Of course August was nearly always wet, but in
the golden days of memory the sun shone through-
out the year. The Emerald Isle gets its colour from
the caressing strokes of the warm rain, and its
lushness from the Gulf Stream that embraces the
whole of Ireland. In the dry periods dew drops
sparkle the small fields, and shine the stone walls.
For us at Ballymartin – almost an island on its own –
the colour from our bedroom windows was of the
blue-grey-green of the sea, and from the bathroom

and kitchen windows the changing pink shadows of the grey-purple mountains. Honeysuckle Lane was also seen from the back of the house, its pathway to the mountains all part of the collective mystique. It was known to us as Ghostie. Did those long-gone wander back and forth happy still in the connection?

'Us', Peggy, as well you know, consisted of you, your brother Warren, my brother Mike, and myself. We were self-contained, needed no friends and saw parents as a backdrop to the fiercely imaginative lives we led together. You were the boss, and the eldest, Mike, the deputy, next in age. Warren and I both younger and more obedient. On the periphery of this little quartet was your much younger brother Paul, who was too young to be included in such a positive-thinking group. Incidentally, children can be very unkind. Your mother, my tactless and unimaginative aunt, had informed Paul early in his life that he was an unwanted afterthought. So Paul played at being not wanted to the limit of his developing cunning. This 'babe' knew how to rile us, and when he caught the four of us, the elder two just into their teens, smoking up Ghostie, he said that if we didn't let him smoke too he'd tell Uncle James.

When I wrote my first book *My Father's House* the memory of Father was of a brilliant but humble, eccentric man. What I'm unlocking now is a picture of a fierce dynamo who would dish out punishment on the spot, forget the whole incident in minutes, and generally make the sun shine again. Sulks and resentment were not allowed in our household. It's only now I'm accepting that the various aspects made up the whole person.

Your mother had a tongue like forked lightning, saved only by the blessed Irish humour, which in her case was manifest in the huge rumbling outbursts of laughter that had their base in her stomach. A stomach that grew larger and larger with the years. It's interesting that these two, brother and sister, should explode into expression of feeling. My mother, as you know, never exploded, except for the red colour flushing her face, the poor lady unable to sweat – 'perspire' I think they called it then. She believed sweat was for the common folk until she realized that her daughter broke into little beads of it at the sight of Grandmother pushing her spectacles to the end of her nose and peering over the top.

Your father, our Uncle Humphrey, would sit on the sidelines watching the fierce battles between his wife and daughter, and saying to Father: 'Give me fierce cats any day to a tame mouse.' You took issue about any instruction or order that didn't appeal to your own type of logic: 'All right. Try and make me.' You spent a certain amount of time in your bedroom, sent there by your mother when she felt she might be losing the argument, and in there you'd make effigies of her which you could destroy. In later years Paul referred to her as 'the auld bitch'. Indulgence in hatred of your mother united you and Paul. Warren never saw her like that, but then he was the favourite, and in any case Warren had his own built-in rose-coloured spectacles.

You found it difficult to forgive your father for not standing up for you, but in later years have understood his enjoyment of the battle.

Uncle Humphrey was quite old when you were born, but the point about him was not that he was an elderly parent, rather that he was a life-enhancer with his enthusiasm for living.

One year you were all staying with us in Scotland when Warren got stuck at the top of one of our tall beech trees. He was trying to see into a rook's nest when one leg slipped. Shouts from you – and your father was sprinting across the lawn, leaping up the tree, and with one arm round his son, balancing, he jumped onto the soft bed of leaves beneath. The circle of admiring family was to remember this when, in even older age, he took to shaking his pipe on to the carpet and spitting into the fire.

One of the great traditions in Ulster, both Protestant and Catholic, is for all members of each denomination to go to church, in view of each other, to swell the numbers. In our case to sit in the two front rows in the Presbyterian church in Kilkeel. Men and boys wearing dark suits, hair smalmed down; women and girls in their best hats and dresses.

Your hat, Peggy, was a severe Panama, chosen by your mother, while you dreamed of multi-coloured dresses and large party hats, preparing for the sharp pronounced colours you were to wear when you had your own account. I, on the other hand, loving the Panama, had to hide, scowling, under a straw hat with flowers round the brim, which, according to my gentle feminine mother, was what pretty blonde little girls wore.

The two congregations would have been praising the same Lord, and conceiving Him separately as a good Protestant or Catholic.

The humourless minister of our church had a way of leaning on the pulpit, fixing his gaze – so it seemed – on us, and in a hoarse stage-whisper asking: 'Which of you have been in the closet today?' He had a fond way of addressing himself to the little room we were all supposed to enter for contemplation and prayer. Grandmother would break her rule about sweets being allowed only after breakfast on Saturdays, by passing peppermints under the pew to stifle the giggles.

Our Church never gave us any impression other than that we were élitist Protestants, giving no thought to any other group, mainly because we never met them.

Yes, Peggy, you who are in a hospital bed slightly in pain, but lightly asleep, remember, along with myself, that in those childhood days our only problems were around the subject of pocket money, and would there be enough to buy a few cigarettes between the four of us, along with the sweets. If you'd known then what a pernicious habit it was to become for you you would not have practised inhaling so lightheartedly. If the parents had problems they were not discussed with us. Grandmother took care of all household arrangements. As a background to our activities we'd occasionally hear the word 'troubles' and we'd know it was in connection with the IRA, that band of rebels whom we guessed to be exciting and who invaded the lives of those who got in their way. We took care not to be hanging about in their way – whatever their way was.

'Cold-blooded murderers.'

'Yes Peggy.'

Nuala is in the room again, saying: 'Did you ever see the like of it?' as we watch you pull yourself up into a sitting – commanding – position, your eyelids fluttering, but you can't remember what else you have to say.

The nurse has been more or less allocated to you, Dr Peggy Fry. She came about a week ago bringing in your breakfast of tea and blancmange. You sipped once, then lay back, and Nuala with her arms around your shoulders lifted you oh so carefully: 'Sure there's nothing of the girl', and, smiling broadly, added: 'You'll be from the old country?' Your eyes opened, and this time with those dark grey-green ocean depths you actually observed her. I saw her through your eyes, she with her red hair tied back in a deep purple ribbon, and her nurse's uniform stuck around with pins, safety pins, scissors, and, incongruously, some calendar, which on closer inspection was seen to be for race-meetings.

She said again: 'Where are you from?' And you from the depth of the bed managed: 'Ulster.'

'Faith, you can't help that,' said she, straightening the bedclothes and giving you a gentle pat. And as she went out into the corridor we could hear the sounds of: '*In a mean abode/On the Shankhill Road/ Lived a man called William Bloat/He had a wife/curse of his life/who continually got his goat/So, one day at dawn/with her night-dress on/he cut her bloody throat.*'

You smile.

Father had made his decision mid-stream at Queen's, Belfast, to get out of Ulster. He hoped he was leaving bigotry and prejudice behind. He transferred to Edinburgh University to complete his MA, and to start his lifelong love affair with Scotland. On graduation he went as an assistant to the great Revd Norman Macleod in Dumbartonshire, and from there, via the 1914–18 war, to Galloway, the rolling hills of which I saw as the object of 'I shall lift up mine eyes unto the hills.'

The idea of Father going to war was something Mother and I found difficult to handle. He joined the King's Own Scottish Borderers and was soon promoted to Major, and no one in the regiment knew that 'Paddy' – the name given to all the Irish – was in fact a Presbyterian minister. Father was fascinated by the strategy and tactics of war. The Ten Commandments were probably not at the forefront of his mind when battle commenced. We were grateful that he never wore his military medals on his clerical robes when in the pulpit on, say, Armistice Day. He commanded the local Home Guard, and if there had to be an exercise on Sunday he wore his uniform hidden under his clerical robes. The village accepted all this because, wasn't it wartime? And Irish clergymen can be just as unpredictable as others of his country.

Mother and I had to watch generals of the Boer, Crimea and Great War come to attention to salute their diminutive commander, Major The Revd James Fisher. Under Father's command the Home Guard was no Dad's Army.

Atmosphere at the Manse of Crossmichael was not so lighthearted as it was at Ballymartin. The house with its thirteenth-century foundations pushed history out between the cracks, and latched on to the vivid imagination that was in most of us. Once, when you, Peggy, were staying with us, we had visions following a film we had been take to see in Castle Douglas.

Gabriel Over the White House was about the Angel Gabriel giving inspiration to a failing American president, and, as far as we were concerned Gabriel was outside our bedroom window that night disguised as an owl. The darkness that was around the Manse took silence as its accomplice, and any sound coming from it was both mystical and frightening. Our fear, Peggy, became terror, until, thank God, the very real bubbling and gurgling of the pipes all round the house brought back normality.

I've thought since about the versatility of the Angel Gabriel, of how Mohammed, simple shepherd that he was, out there minding his flock – and probably his own business – was confronted by this apparition which spoke enough words to him to make into a book. For Islam, *The Book*. Now, if you're going to measure the likelihood of the world's religious beliefs being actual, you can't do much better than weigh up the likelihood of virgin births and bodily assumptions and illiterate shepherds taking dictation from an angel.

The Manse, large and sprawling, was, I was sure, a playground for the departed; they with their invisibility who can walk through walls. In my adult years some of my nightmares have been placed in the Manse, and those walking about in it have been strangers.

Night-time led me down a long corridor to the smallest and coldest bedroom in the house. The only room that had any warmth was the upstairs bathroom. The belching and gurgling water tank was more of a comfort to me than the little night light by my bed which created frightening shadows on the walls, the shapes turning into humans coming ever nearer.

In later years, when I'd written out some of my threatening fantasies into childhood poems, Mother and I used to go into the bathroom for consultations of a female nature, one on the low nursing chair with a blue velvet seat, the other – me – perched on the high bath with elegant legs. I think it was in there that I learned that Father Christmas was not the frightening man who would come down my chimney, but my comforting mother; and it was also in there that I learned that babies were not found under gooseberry bushes – of all prickly places – but came out of mothers' stomachs, one of hundreds of eggs having been put there by fathers.

'So do we come out of eggs like baby birds?'

'Well . . . um . . .'

At Ballymartin mine was also the smallest of the rooms, but it was sandwiched between the parents' and Mike's. I could lie in bed in the morning – except that children never willingly do – and watch the early sunlight make shining saucers on the sea. Seagulls soared, and down the road in front of our house came the men in carts, driven by either a mule or a donkey, calling out: 'Herrin' alive. Lovely fresh herrin'.' And fresh they were, pearly fresh, with Mary or Annie going out with a large dish, counting the pennies, and watching the fish slither onto the plate, blank white eyes staring. The gamble at breakfast would be:

'What have you got?'

'Soft roe.'

'Good. Let's swop.'

Mother and Mike liked the soft roes and Father and I the hard.

No sooner was breakfast over than there would be the race to the one downstairs loo, from where you could sit and look at the Mourne Mountains, or, if you were Father, and there were guests in the house, to read the *Daily Telegraph*.

The walk to the bank head was to assess the position of the tide. Watching the tide was a very serious matter, and in later life I've seen men tap barometers in the hall with the same enquiring dedication. When the tide was out we bathed at the Point Sands. The Sands was so called because the rocks to the left from where we stood stretched in diminishing size towards a large one on which could be seen a cormorant or a seal, and as the tide turned, the rocks, bird and animal disappeared. It was our jealously guarded private world. We could not countenance anyone else on the beach, except perhaps the old woman who would come down for the seaweed when the tide had gone out, strands of it lingering. But though the beach was our territory, our real bathing was from the Black Rock, from which we could dive.

We were told that the old woman was probably a relation. There were relations everywhere, from one who married into the family of the Earls of Kilmorey, to those who lived in small white cottages with thatched roofs — wild dogs to guard them — to the redheaded family near us at Ballymartin whose appearance gave off the aura of Huguenot of which we were all supposed to be a part. We didn't know them very well, they in their smaller houses. The tightly fashioned security of our little world provided us with an unconscious air of superiority. It is the conscious part of that feeling that is being attacked in Northern Ireland today.

Sunday afternoon was the day when the family from all over County Down came to visit The Revd Uncle James and his family. Those that worked had to come at weekends, and those who were not working probably thought a Sunday was the appropriate day. The small driveway became packed with cars — all in those days looking like large hen coops on wheels —

the fuchsia growing miraculously out of the wall round the garden and blooming pillar-box red. Turning into the drive the visitors could already smell the hot butter of baking. There would be mounds and mounds of pancakes from the griddle and, on each, granulated sugar and farm butter. Father would have mowed the lawn, some of the cars lapping over onto it, and none of us minding that our cricket pitch would be changed again the following day.

These tall striking relations had come perhaps for a bathe, but certainly for a good gossip, and never touching on the Troubles, because for them in their comfortable houses with maids rattling about in the back premises, nothing unpleasant hovered near their doorsteps. Strictly speaking the pancakes were for the bathers, a reward for plunging into the sea of ice, but with Grandfather's death a certain sternness had disappeared, discipline relaxing with the softening up of Grandmother. I don't remember cakes, Peggy, but I think you were right to remind me it was always a square tin of sweet biscuits, consumed at a sitting. I have one of them still in my kitchen, a faded Yuletide picture of Christmas in Belfast, a horse and coach through the snow, elegant clothes and telling its own story of a once-upon-a-time peace and well-being.

Your family stayed away on Sundays; they liked to have us to ourselves. So instead, you and Warren – sometimes Paul with his nurse whom he call Aah – swam in Kilkeel harbour, diving in beside the boats and the oil and shells from the Dublin Bay prawns –

prawns which we knew were netted near Kilkeel. On really cold days, we were driven to Warrenpoint to the baths, the taste in the mouth strange after the iced seawater of Ballymartin. Warrenpoint – the eye of the storm, a storm that would sometimes rage between the giants on their mountains, each on his own side of the border, Finn McCool on the Ulster side the more famous, the stronger. Warrenpoint – where darts of sunlight escaping the clouds would light up the small town, an invitation to all. The border not far away, the smuggling, the occasional sound of a shot, perhaps early warnings that Warrenpoint would become a target for some of the nastier acts of terrorism.

You and Mike would practice your high diving into the pool, Paul jumping from the top divingboard, while Warren and I, both plump in those days, slipped porpoise-like from the shallow end. But it was a tame bathe compared with Ballymartin.

Until you have had the experience of diving into the Irish Sea you don't know what shock is. It's not so much a taking of the breath, it's more that the breath gets strangled in the throat. Poor Mother having watched the blue shivering bodies surface, was eventually pushed in by Father. Her dithering over the years had been acceptable while it was unnecessary to set an example. Once the children were there, Father's patience ran out – so pushed she was, and when feelings of shock and hurt pride were overcome she experienced the sharp thrill that comes with the first surfacing. It does not mean that she came to like it. She never did. And 'furthermore', as the minister in the Kilkeel church kept repeating, she began an understanding that there is something a little unpredictable in the Irish.

The swimming test came for each member of the family at the age of seven. A swim from the Black Rock to what we called The Battery had to be achieved without any floating on the back, or anything so demeaning as a rubber ring. It was quarter of a mile and it was swim – or else!

Warren, our lovely Warren, of the sweet nature and the well-disguised brilliance – who was killed in a car crash in Egypt just at the war's end – was, we thought, really a fish. Of the four elements water was his. Long after others were out of the water shivering in towels and picking small stones out from between their toes, he would be lying at the point where sea met sand in a state of fat ecstasy. Not one other in your family, Peggy, seemed to mind that Warren was everyone's favourite. He must have arrived into this world ready to like and be liked. During the war he was an airman doctor, once again loved by all. There was a massive RAF funeral for him, but it didn't bring him back to us.

I don't think your family ever quite recovered from his death. When Aunt Netta heard the news she said: 'I wish it had been you.' Well, of course you never forgave her. How could you? But now that the doctors have found consoling medicine for you, you're more comfortable and have asked for her once or twice. You've also asked if Warren has been, and I say 'Yes' because I'm not sure if 'No' would be quite right.

Ballymartin village in those days was hardly even a hamlet. The actual village was up the hill and out of sight. Our house was on its own except for a smallholding nearby where a Catholic family called Rogers concentrated on looking after their goats, their cows, their small productive fields, and the business of having children. The girls had names after the saints, and the boys' names came straight out of the Bible. A quarter of a mile in the other direction was the Rogers' shop. In Scotland it would have been called the 'wee shop', in England it would have been called the 'corner shop', but in Ballymartin it was 'go down to Rogers and get me a pound of butter'.

As it happened, most of the farmers round and about, complete in their whitewashed cottages, thatched roofs, pecking hens, threatening dogs, grunting pigs, a cow or two, made their own butter. *And* buttermilk. We got through pounds of butter, and the milk we drank seemed to be straight from the cow's udder. Sterilization? Not on your life. One or two calcified TB glands around my neck and shoulders have caused the Well Woman Clinics to have a thought or two.

When Mother first came to Ulster she was not allowed to know this somewhat wild looking woman who came to the back door carrying milk in a can and the bright yellow butter in a basket, the product of all the fertility round about. Mother had been taken first to our Uncle Frank's house, called Rowana, in County Meath, a small Georgian, with a maid to answer the door. There was a certain air of delicacy here, and Mother was to be broken in through the more affluent members of the family. Uncle Frank's eccentric stinginess did not hit her until later. It was only as time went on and Mother came face to face with the large handsome women from the farm that she answered her own question: yes, they probably were related – but only through marriage came the echo of her mother's voice. What today may have to be spelt out is that relationship was only acknowledged with the Protestant households – and it has to be admitted, to take it one further, that Catholics were for employment only. Except, that is, for the Rogers. The Catholic maids could go as often as they liked to Mass – and they did – the lying and thieving was not diminished, so everyone said.

'What do you think he does, sitting there by the sliding panel in the church? I mean what do you think he's really giving his mind to as he repeats automatic phrases?'

'His laundry list, and did he remember to give it to his housekeeper.'

Perhaps it was your curiosity about the thinking of the Catholic priests that led you to have your own confessional box in your role as a psychoanalyst. It took you seven years of full analysis for yourself – on top of your doctor of medicine degree – that added insight to professionalism.

'Mike too,' say you. 'Also a paid listener.'

A lovely family solicitor in the heart of London is what he is today. Plenty of people there wanting to hear themselves think out loud, and Mike sitting behind a large leather desk, an unlit pipe in the ashtray, and the files up to the ceiling dropping swathes of ancient dust if anyone moves suddenly.

I suppose it was feeding the abundant energy and appetite of you that increased the journeys to the farm, the calling in of the butcher's van and the fishmonger's.

'More please,' you'd say, throwing the food down your throat, each mouthful chasing the next, stoking the boiler for the adventures of the day, your hand thrust out with the plate.

'Come on, come on,' minutes later to us, as you jumped over one of the dining-room chairs blocking the way to the door, the food rolling about in your stomach, but making room for the ice-cream you'd be eating at Rogers' in about an hour.

Appetite is failing you now as you sip, and then spill, and then sip something that looks like liquid blancmange. But there's a secret inside of you that we are supposed to guess of the double nature of what's going on. And there's the question, perhaps, of who is it you're waiting for. Because, Peggy, as the physical strength ebbs, so the spirit of you gains momentum, and the energy that comes from that is for remembering – and the filling in of history.

The miracle of soil, water and air that is the Irish potato was described recently by an Irish writer who had given the potato a place of honour when describing a literary dinner: there it was, feather-like upon a plate, steaming. This writer has the same gift as you of pulling meaning out of people's conversations long before they've come – grindingly – to the point.

'Yes, yes . . . and then?' Hurry, hurry, there may be a boat to catch, a train to climb aboard, a life to save.

'What did she say?' Mother would often turn to me, but you would be through the front door, jumping all six steps down, and calling, once again: 'Come on. Come on', as we were hurrying after you to Rogers' shop, a sixpenny piece in each hot hand, it being Saturday morning.

You went rushing into your first day-school, tumbling your companions in fun, understood what you were being told, and firing individual questions at the teachers: 'Why does a train make more noise if you're standing under a bridge than if you're standing beside it?' In time you rushed over to Penrose College, a boarding-school in Wales, dispelled any ideas of the fecklessness of the Irish, but possibly confirming belief that sometimes imagination got in the way of fact. Soon you were in charge of the costumes for the school plays, until a scholarship took you to Queen's University, even though you were not yet clear which of your talents you could syphon into a career. You began as an art student, taking drawings of your costume designs to the art master, and suggesting you could make more, and especially for the poor creature who was sitting naked in the middle of the room.

You decided that the fellow art students were stuck in their tubes of paint, and changed to become a medical student. Medical students were up to your speed, and the like-minded editing of speech, and the twinkle in the eye that was to do with sex; but you were keeping yourself for an altogether more important encounter that was – unknown to you – already in the making. You came out from Queen's top of the year, and to follow went Warren, who also topped his year.

The Protestant Ulsterman is impressed by professionalism and the capacity for work, so two of Father's brothers were defending these shores – British and Irish – in the army and the navy. One was in medicine, two in law, and the youngest, Johnnie, who died before we could know him – a favourite of the Irish gods, the greedy gods always taking the best for themselves – took a rowing crew one year from Newry to the Henley Regatta.

'Where's Newry?'

'God knows. In the bush somewhere.'

Actually, in the bogs.

Aunt Berta, married to Uncle Alec, the solicitor, was intimidating, with her straight back and deep voice. But admire her we did, good-looking woman that she was. Complete with four children she made a temporary move to Dublin, to Trinity, to take a medical degree. Of course she nearly succeeded, but in the end bad health took her away. Her two daughters, Margaret and Dorothy, became solicitors, one son, Lex, a professor of English, and the other son, Bertie, a baker.

Sometimes we were invited into Aunt Berta's kitchen in their house, Coolbawn, in Warrenpoint, a huge room with copper pots round the walls, and there would Aunt Berta be, stirring the deep yellow lemon curd, herself in a thin, long yellow dress, the colour blending in with the copper pots and the whole a lasting memory of sunlight.

Most of the Fisher wives were strong, and ruled their husbands, the husbands seeming to enjoy the release from domestic decisions, business and a men's world appealing most: sailing boats, merchant ships, rowing boats, lined up for sport. The exception was James, our father, who was more cerebral, and when other brothers were starting to allow their wives to redecorate their houses, Father would be creating more and more book shelves to line the walls.

I'm not sure if the men made loving husbands. Dutiful, reliable, loyal, but I don't think the fashion was to understand women's ways. Father simply ruled everything to do with the shaping of our lives, and, in later years, quite a lot of the affairs of Scotland.

Old sepia family photographs show a massive tribe of us, but thank God they did not all come to stay at Ballymartin, because Grandmother would have put the families two to a room. She would have been all right, she with her bedroom to herself, and her green-hooded deck chair isolated in the shade.

I'm not the first to wonder if there isn't quite a bond between the Irish and the Jews. Family comes first. And the Mafia, now I come to think about it. You'll agree that we are interested in each other, even when we are doing dull things. But then an Irishman – and I'm going to annoy my Ulster family on insisting on the word – can never tell a dull story because even if the substance is opaque the embellishments are not, and like the rolling stone it will have gathered much moss on the way.

The great oral tradition has not died out. Word of mouth. It's a graphic description. I can see how with ease today the various denominations, creeds, groups, parties, talk to the press and media. Flow, flow. It's a job to get in your word. But, of course, when we were young there were no Dimblebys, nor David Frost for that matter. Even they have difficulty with the flood. When the British soldiers in the last century were commanded to take the English language to the Irish, they'd sit in an ill-lit cottage on the West coast wondering at the sight of impoverished Ireland: they with old sacks on their backs rather than the expense of clothes, a jar of poteen in their hands, and talking and talking, quoting and quoting – Homer, Ovid, Yeats, Joyce – the words coming out of their mouths free of embarrassment, free of need to make reference, perhaps not quite knowing if they themselves were inventing, and giving the intruders the very politest 'get the hell out of here'. And looking out through the hole in the wall that was supposed to be their window and wondering how many more of the English soldiers were on their way.

Ireland thinks about the twentieth century, but *feels* the past and the present together. What *was*, *is*.

You got it right, Peggy, when you smirked at the attempt to turn Ireland communist.

'As if anyone would pay attention to the System.'

Well, they've outlasted communism, and much more besides; they'll be their own people, down, down the ages – those that are left of them. It's difficult to know if the killing will stop; perhaps only if the fight in the head ceases, and of course emotion can be in the fist.

The first little trip Mother made to the Rogers' shop was to buy butter on a day when conditions outside were too severe for the journey to the farm. She pushed the door open gingerly, for she'd seen Mrs Rogers from a distance and was wary. She was wary of so much. She'd been handed over to her husband by her mother and had never even bought a pair of gloves for herself without Grannie Pawling being present. Grannie Pawling made *entrances* into shops, houses, theatres, the very emblem of patronage. So, when 'good morning Madam' was replaced with 'It's Yourself then. Come away in, girl dear, out of the rain', Mother forgot the cast of her mother. But like most of the timid of the world she was strong on obstinacy and prejudice, as was to be seen by her attitude towards my German car.

She loved your speed, Peggy, and your speech,

and the joint knowledge that she didn't have to listen to you as she could not understand a word you were saying:

'Sure-it-was-great-in-the-water-today and a-crab-caught-me-between-the-toes and we're-ready-for-tea-now and the-hot-butter-of-them.'

'Yes, yes, Peggy, but it is not butter you put on a sting,' and you flinging your arms round her hips, because you were so small, and she so tall, and both of you into the dining-room, the flow from you continuing.

If ever I've *seen* a cliché it was there in the cottage-loaf figure of Mrs Rogers. Black, black hair piled high (nothing Anglo-Saxon here), head attached to the body, free of a neck and somewhere at the base of this large frame two fat feet. But sketched on this particular face was an intelligence that was not disguised by the cottage-loaf smile. It did not surprise us that all seven children 'did well for themselves'.

Once over the impact of the greeting, Mother spotted the intelligence, and the whole aura of the woman filled the spare corners of this excitingly congested small shop. They shook hands, and Mother, who had been brought up in a nursery presided over by a nanny, and far from the comforting clasp of a mother, felt a reassurance that all was going to be well.

'It'll be the butter you're wanting on this bad day,' Mrs Rogers beamed, and reaching beneath the counter of the shop – her huge frame taking up even more of the limited space – she came up again, triumphant. There inside a chamber pot where a pattern of climbing roses adorned the sides were several carefully wrapped pounds of butter, the shape of them long and thin like a canoe.

Rogers' had not been on the agenda when Father told Mother of some of the aspects of Ireland she might find strange. However having made the discovery herself she told Father that she would go to Rogers' in future for the butter. Father didn't disagree with her, but sliding his glance in our direction, he knew that on the first dry day Mike and I would be up the lane to the farm. He may have understood that we were testing our courage against the farm dogs.

When I consider the shortage of butter in the last war, and when, today, I listen to the media extolling the virtues of a non-fat diet, I wonder in awe at the quantities of butter consumed by us at Ballymartin.

There were two fond favourites who came delivering to the door. One, the baker, who came all the way from Belfast – about 45 miles – in his red van, the name INGLIS all over it, stopped with us longer than most, not because we had come bounding out of the house with eager arms into the trays of iced buns with little buttons of sugar on top, but because Annie, swaying down the front steps of the house had an 'I'm approachable' look in her eye that most of the van drivers fancied. Annie flirted with all tradesmen. She cared little that the man might, indeed, attend the Catholic church – though, shame to tell, our tradesmen were all Protestant. It would not have occurred to a driver from a Catholic-owned shop to stop at the house of The Revd James Fisher. 'Let people be' was Annie's motto – for it gave herself endless scope as she set forth into each day, her bottom waggling.

The other favourite tradesman was the butcher, Danny. He would come to Ballymartin in his white van, his blue and white striped apron smeared with blood, and talk and talk to his customers, time appearing to have no consequence, and his face as red as the meat he cut, and a voice that would carry over the mountains. He had two beautiful grey-hounds, which he raced. I don't believe he needed to be his own van driver, but the chat was what counted, and our family, though originally from Ulster, came with news from 'over there'. Sometimes he'd ask: 'What do they think of us over there?' and not caring that much, but hoping there might be the seeds of a fight in it. Father equalled Danny: both knew how far they could go in raising moral issues, and they'd stand and talk, and stand and talk and argue and talk, until it was long past time for putting the joint into the old black range.

One day the conversation was more prolonged than usual, the two men out of sight behind the open door of the van, when the sound of breaking glass and damaged metal reached Mother in the sitting-room. White in the face, her feet hurrying, she came through the front door, believing the worst. James was nowhere to be seen, but there was a pile-up on the road.

'The Lord only knows what the hurry is these days,' Danny was saying, and Mother, stopping in her tracks, heard Father say: 'I doubt it.'

The whole of our little area of the village of Ballymartin turned out to assist in the clearing-up of the mess, and, as one said to another: 'It's not even as if one of the goats was on the road.'

A Rogers boy had come out from a side road on his bicycle, and, without looking, tried to cross the main road. Words flew as some tried to make sense of the happening, but as there was no speed limit or insurance of cars, hardly even a licence for driving, the matter had to be settled there and then. Money changed hands with the car driver, an agreement was reached about not getting the 'polis', the car went limping down the road, and Joey Rogers, on his bicycle, was by then out of sight.

There was one particular cloth-capped victim of Annie's who sat each evening on the bank across the road. And it wasn't long before Annie had me walking with her, up and down the road, ever closer to the man, he making his own assessment as he talked to his cronies. Each time that we passed he said: 'Good evening.' Except that in Ireland you don't just say 'Good evening' and leave it at that, you add to it a little ditty that paints the picture: 'Good evening. Sure it's warm enough to take the nose off a snipe, so it is.'

One of the facets that *was* on Father's agenda for an introduction to Ireland was the dropping of the afternoon. At 12 o'clock noon the day shifts into

evening. Whatever happened to the poor old afternoon you might wonder. After all, it's not as if they
could have forgotten about afternoon, because the
Irish, if nothing else – and there is plenty else – do
not forget. So 'Good evening' and 'Good evening' it
was as we passed up and down.

Annie became pregnant in the end; it was the year
the cat came with us, and she may have confided the
rendezvous to the cat, because at the end of August,
fat cat and fat maid had to face the future. The
kittens were all drowned in a bucket by Annie, and
Annie went home for a week. When she returned
she was concave and her mother had another mouth
to feed. Down at the working level of life in those
days practicality took over sometimes from expected
behaviour. Men saw to it that they *could* get their
women pregnant before marriage. Our Annie out-
witted them all because she did not marry until she
was long past the period of breeding.

In our part of Scotland, young couples would
come down to the Manse to be married. It was
putting on side if you were merely from the village,
and not part of the farming community, to be married
in church. Father put on all his robes and conducted
a full service in his study; occasionally Mother sang,
and we were confined to the nursery because of our
tendency to snigger; Oats would scratch at the door
because something was going on in there and he was
left out of it. The nursery suited us fine because it
looked onto the front door and Mike and I could
take bets on the shape of the bride coming up to it.

I was approaching my teens when Annie first invited me to join the evening parade at Ballymartin. She may have seen the glint in my own eye, and the dawning awareness of just why men were different. The seeding of a novelist was taking place inside me, which may have given the necessary, but detached – and exciting – encounters a double edge. How Annie actually became pregnant was still a mystery. Twelve-year-old girls were told nothing, but the smiles and careful observations from the men allowed me to indulge in fantasy, and to bask in Annie's fun.

You might wonder, Peggy, why Father didn't put a stop to the 'evening' parade, he with his dislike of the baring of private parts, and his biblical belief in the sanctity of marriage. The answer as I see it today is that, at heart, hidden behind his reading of the *Daily Telegraph*, Father was something of a socialist. Walking up and down the road with one's maid was in his eyes a social function, and perhaps it made up for the bedtime insult of having the 'servants' sleep in the boiler-room.

Your Aunt Marj, Peggy, was no socialist, and every now and again would say, in her mother's voice: 'Things aren't what they used to be', and Father would say: 'For whom?'

It may have been the budding author in me that took me to sleep in the boiler-room one night, and I'm glad now I did, because the room gave window through gently swaying trees onto the Mourne Mountains.

We can see through windows now, Peggy, but onto a London scene of swaying trees scattering the dust, the birds beneath taking on the same colouring.

You're restless in your bed and I wonder if for the time being you've thought enough about Bally-martin. You lift your arm slowly off the bed and attempt to stretch it towards the door, and, yes, Nuala is coming into the room, and sees the welcome you are giving her.

'You *will* let him in,' you say, and Nuala, glancing towards me says: 'Whatever the dear girl wants.'

There's a small gold chain showing round Nuala's neck, the uniform partly obscuring it, and you and I know that it's attached to a crucifix. Not the simple gold of the cross, but the writhing agony of the Saviour.

'And Himself he could not save,' say you.

Nuala sits still. She fingers the crucifix, and lovingly pops it beneath the starched white uniform.

'I'll tell you when prejudice began for me,' I say, nervously looking at Nuala. 'With the Ballymartin priest averting his eyes from us in our bright Sunday clothes and our grinning faces.'

We try a laugh together.

'Everything about him stood for dejection: his black hat, his black suit, his care-worn boots.'

'And Mary in the kitchen, comfortable in her prejudice, saying: "Now don't you be talking to the likes of him. He'll put a spell on yous."'

'How come that clerics dress in mournful black when the Lord was, and is, The Light of the World?'

'Catholicism,' say you with more strength in your voice than I've heard for a time or two.

Nuala is now bustling round the room, smiling to herself, and saying: 'What hope have they in Northern Ireland when the likes of you carry on this way?'

Picking up a pillow that you've managed to get onto the floor, Nuala leans over to talk quietly to you: 'I'll be away for a day, Peg-a-Leg, having a rest from you,' and you loving the daring of this highly-trained nurse, say: 'Don't forget to bring me some fags.'

You sink into sleep where no one can reach you, and I remember the cigarette, snatched from my bag, when we were beside the mountains contemplating Slieve Binian on our last visit, and the paroxysm of coughing when you lit up, and my foot on the accelerator, my hand snatching the cigarette from you, and you shouting 'I can do what I want with my own life', the car swerving to miss a wandering and very woolly sheep, and thoughts of the delicious leg of lamb that was to be for lunch going from us as the car headed for the hospital.

Shall I talk to Nuala about the Pope, and about your uncle, The Revd James Fisher – my father? About Father's broadmindedness once he'd met some of the saintly priests out on the battlefront at Arras in the Great War, administering to the very sick and dying, but forever the crucifix held in one hand? Shall I ask Nuala if the plain cross wouldn't – would – be better?

It was from Mary, Peggy, we learned about this

terrible old man – or was he God? – the Pope. Why did he have a capital P like G for God? We were not certain if he were God or man. He lived in something called the Vatican, had an army of his own, and would come and get us if we weren't good. But in fairness to Father we must remember that even before the war, and before his encounter with what he called the Christian side of Catholicism, he'd left Ulster, possibly because of fear of his own prejudice. We must also remember that he returned at least once a year for the rest of his life. Was it to remind himself of the prejudice he hoped he'd left there? Your mother, Peggy, hung onto both her prejudice and her bigotry, as garments around her.

Nuala is reading my mind. 'Did you see the picture of the Holy Father, white handkerchief held high, leading some of his flock to safety in Derry?'

'Yes, Nuala, I did.'

But you're right, Peggy, we had no Catholic friends. You couldn't say that the Rogers were actually friends, though we probably saw more of them than any others. The seven children were in various stages of development, so, wherever we were, and whatever we were doing, there would be a Rogers. In the early years I thought Mrs Rogers was a gypsy, but as she got older and her black hair went grey, I could sense something atavistic about her, with her umbilical cord attached both to the soil and to the distant past. Joey, our contemporary, lives in the same house he grew up in, with his own family. I saw him a few years back when I drove from

Rostrevor along the coast, the mountains on my left, to Ballymartin. As I came slowly down the hill and turned into 'our' driveway I saw a grey-haired man mending the roof of Rogers house. I even called out: 'D'you know where I can find Joey Rogers?'

He turned fully and smiled, and said: 'Hullo there, Pauline.'

Great tides of warmth washed over me.

I was invited into the house and to their large kitchen, and was handed a cup of tea the colour of amber. The tea brought it all back, as did the hot potato scone and the bright yellow farm butter, and I'm handing it now to you as the gift that it was, because the room is full suddenly of the smell of fresh Irish baking. We can inhale and look at Joey's face, and through him back to his mother, and we can see the long-ago pride and the intelligence that came from her.

We hardly touched on the Troubles, Joey and I, though I had to ask if they were affected – only a number of miles away from two bad areas.

'Faith, they wouldn't dare,' he laughed, and changed the subject.

He asked about you, and about Mike, and he knew about Warren. We remembered the boat trips at night out to sea to get mackerel and herring. We were proud that no one was seasick, and that the boys could urinate over the side of the boat, and that the girls could rely on their bladders. Men's talk out at sea, and the dawn coming up on the horizon, shafts of light on land and hitting the mountains, and the sight of mother-of-pearl fish lying in the bottom of the boat.

We shook hands with a warm good-bye, and a question from Joe: 'Will Peggy be back?'

Last year, when illness was coming on you again, I took you to Ballymartin, and we stood and looked at the old house tarted up by some intruder: greenhouses, a garage, flower beds in circles, and the monkey-puzzle, and fuchsia in the walls, gone. You wept a tear, and when we managed to get you down to the shore – our shore – there were people on it, leaving their litter as they walked, and others bathing, diving into the sea from our special ledge in the Black Rock.

Climbing carefully over the rock we went in particular to the part that opened up to receive the sea, which we called the gulf. We remembered visions of Mike, his thin body leaning into the wind, stick in his hand orchestrating the waves, the ice-green water erupting, the spray almost into the heavens, and we both laughed. I took you to tea with Joey Rogers, and you and he settled down to your third cup of tea and with one of your many, many cigarettes, and Joey saying: 'Sure, you'll kill yourself, Peggy,' and I sitting across the table, looking, and knowing.

World War II took Mike out of the country, as it did you and Warren. You, Peggy, emerged from it with an illegitimate child, your strongest gesture yet against your mother. Mike came out slightly damaged by a bad dose of measles through doing a kindness to a distressed child in North Africa during the Italian landings. Mike has been doing kindnesses ever since. Warren, as we know, did not come out of it at all, and I emerged with a broken shoulder-blade and leg from crashing an ambulance when driving it to pick up a paratrooper who had literally fallen from the sky. On wet leaves, going round a corner, in this light high-sided American ambulance, vehicle and driver took off and rolled down a bank. I ended up in the same hospital as the heap of bones that was the remains of the soldier.

Next to me in the hospital ward, the curtains all around her, was an ATS girl who had been on a train, corridorless, when some soldiers began to plague and abuse her. In desperation she opened the carriage door, on the rail side, and was more or less cut apart by a passing train. It's strange, isn't it, how a series of chance happenings can lead – well, yes, let's say it – to a changed point of view. And I'm telling you now, that it was my first introduction to the loving side of Catholicism, as I sensed the priest and the nuns who sat by her bed willing her – with God's help – back to life, but, if not, letting her know it would be all right. The priest seemed a very long way from the shuffling priestly question-marks of Ulster.

I convalesced in the house of an adopted aunt – in fact the mother of the boyfriend of the moment – and she invited Mother to stay, and Mother was so enchanted with the 'aunt' and the aunt with Mother that in no time at all they were drawing up lists of guests for the wedding, while I, with the plaster removed, was on my way to freedom.

It was difficult for you, Peggy, when you returned from Singapore pregnant. You had to leave the Air Force in the prime of your medical career, a senior officer in the WAAF, attending to the needs of many. Small you were – are, and tiny in this bed – neat in your uniform, the blue of it finding contact with the blue in your eyes. From time to time an airman had to lift you up so you could see down their throats: 'You're just a little slip of a thing, Ma'am.'

'Says you. Put out your tongue.'

But you met your fate out there: the moon, the night smells, the warmth, the gentle noises, the beauty generally, and you were into the situation that was to alter your life, and which in a way you had been waiting for. He was as quick-witted as yourself, a fellow airman doctor, with the sort of danger about him which women like. He was a 'high-flyer' you wrote to me while it was still a joke. Later you wrote: 'I'm coming home loaded', and I knew it wasn't cash. And then ... Aunt Netta refusing to have you in her flat in Belfast where she'd gone following your father's death – because her bridge friends would not understand. Belfast has had to understand a lot more than that in recent times. You were a whore, she said, and how could you let a man do that to your beautiful little body. Because, if you remember, we were brought up allowed to use our prettiness but never our sexuality. Sex was taboo. So how did we get born?

The first time you were given the intimation that certain parts of the body were all a part of the dirtiness was on the day of Paul's christening. Bored with formal aspects of the party afterwards, you, Mike and Warren went down to the little hut in the bottom of your garden in Kilkeel – a short drive from Ballymartin – and decided to liven things up. Father came down to look for you, and found you and Mike showing each other your 'private parts', while Warren, firm on his little fat feet, was trying to push his penis into the little holes in the garden seat.

Did innocence go from us all following the punishments received, and perhaps with it some of the spontaneity?

One of the attractive aspects of your second house and garden in Kilkeel was its name, Fintamara, and to go with it, almost as if to emphasize the importance of the Gulf Stream, was a palm tree, short and thick and strangely out of place.

There was a frugality to Grandmother's house in Ballymartin which may have been part of the overall plan of outdoor activity. One did not slide across bedrooms on comfortable carpets. You leapt out of bed into a waiting pair of slippers, flew over a wooden floor and rushed down the stairs along a linoleum passage to the only bathroom in the house, and with the loo in it, praying that no one had got there first. The bath, standing on strong legs, was rusted with age, and very often the whole water system came gushing into it, brackish and still part of the mountain streams. Pipes all around the room gurgled and hissed, and the window looked out onto the back area of the house where Mary threw various objects she did not want 'the mistress' to see. Beyond that was Ghostie, and, on dark days, the lane deserving the name it had been given.

There was something almost parsimonious about the emphasis on sea bathing. It was used to save the hot water system – if system is the right word for it. We didn't actually take carbolic soap into the sea because the salt did its job. There were never scented soaps in that bathroom.

Our rich Uncle Frank was the most parsimonious of the lot. He could have had fitted carpets wall to wall. Instead he lived by lighting gas lamps long after electricity had come his way, and he tied up his shoes with string – except on Sundays for church, when he put back in the laces. By the time we were old enough to be properly aware of him, he was still wearing the suit he'd been married in aeons of time before. He deplored waste, detested anyone putting on side. When his son wanted to send *his* son to Cambridge, Uncle Frank asked what was the matter with the Irish universities. Going to Cambridge was definitely putting on side, and it seemed to him a negation of his own son's Ulster education.

It has not always been easy to understand the Protestant Ulsterman's dislike of the English when we're supposed to be on the same side – and in particular the idea of Cambridge and Oxford, and even more the products of the smart English regiments – when their cry has always been allegiance to the Crown.

Uncle Frank was sometimes out of accord with his daughter May, who lived in Dublin and was very much in tune with the expensive dress shops there. Her two little girls were largely brought up by governesses, so their fluent French was a little lost on their grandfather, who thought speaking French and having governesses was definitely putting on side. But I'll give it to the family generally: there's humour there, they're not stingy with that. When poor May was dying in a house her brother and father had rented for her near them in Rostrevor, and when I went to visit her, she spoke little, but opened her eyes as I was leaving, and said: 'No more marriages, Pauline', and the complicity in her eye was the bond between us. But to get back to Uncle Frank, we mustn't forget that he equipped a whole regiment with uniform in the First (ill-named 'Great') World War. Death for one's country is a noble thing, and it was no waste to see the boys were properly clothed.

There was a very small fireplace in the large sitting-room, and I can see him now, close up to it, wearing mittens and looking – one felt almost certain – for the flames. There are times when I've wondered if closeness with money has its root in the Victorian idea of saving up for the rainy day.

'People don't always recognize it when it comes.'

'Oh well done, Peggy, you're awake.' And listening. You've got the defiant look in your eye, and it's going to be sex. The nurses here, the Sister and the Matron, are fascinated, in a way I would not expect from those who see terminal illness all the time, by the suppleness of your body when you are able to move, and the succinctness in your speech when you are able to talk – and the frankness. The Irish accent that your mother tried so hard to suppress has returned, and with it the release from sexual taboos.

You're whispering now, and beckoning me towards you:

'Last night I dreamt I slept with one of the doctors – the one with the limp and the long pale hands, and it was quite nice.'

'Only *quite* nice, Peggy?'

When you talk like this the various colours in your eyes turn to black. Is this a veil, are we prevented from seeing your experience of pain? There's the shadow of a smile, and you say 'McKibben' and you are thinking of the earthy attractiveness of Red & Black Willie. They were big men travelling about in small carts, driven usually by a nodding horse, who, like its masters, saw no need for speed. Their progress down the road was stately, the giant size of them made even greater by the small cart and diminishing horse. They expected cars to get out of their way, which they did because most people in the area were aware of the McKibbens, their sons and their daughters, and *their* sons and daughters. Ulstermen respecting a piece of continuity when they met it.

If you remember, Peggy, our dog Oats who practised some of the habits of the McKibbens, lording it around the garden and grounds of the Manse in Scotland, seeing no reason to change in Ballymartin, defied oncoming cars by staring at them from the middle of the road. One day he stared too long, and was killed outright. It was the single most devastating event of my early years. What was this thing called death that could alter the state of being into a nothingness? Just a limp little body lying on a road. Mike and I wept together, and decided to be on the lookout for death in case it came hovering near our house again.

I suppose an interesting and consoling aspect of personalities is that they leave quite a bit of them-selves behind. In time memory of Oats came with us onto the shore, rushed into the water, dug in the sand (his favourite), upset sand-castles and stayed with us as the vibrant influence he had become. Over death Father was good: it was one of the *facts* that he got into our heads when he considered we were old enough to accept finalities. And I'm sure that stern old Uncle Frank would have approved of that.

We never took another dog to Mourne; the road was going to be the winner in all such incidents. Our short walk each morning to the bank head, dog with us, was interrupted for ever by this intrusion.

One of the great comforting drinks of the world is

buttermilk. It's both a food and an elixir. It leaves little knobs of butter on the side of the glass, and today we still retain the sight of Mary picking up the empty glasses and the jug with the remains, and the remains getting mixed into the wheaten flour, bicarbonate of soda and cream of tartar which becomes soda bread, the quick hands of it telling that the master craftswoman had been at work in the kitchen.

Mary, whose date of birth was never known, died eventually, leaving a sort of warmth behind her, but no clear image of personality. Not so the one to follow her: Bessie. This time she was of the Faith. Attitudes were indeed altering. Grey hair scraped across her brow, two pins holding the curls at the side of her face, she looked out on the world with a defiance and a wisdom. Unbeknown to Father – at least for a time – Bessie read hands and the tea-cups. She didn't mind taking on the future in her calculations of a person's chances, because her closeness to nature gave her the sight, so she said.

Hand-reading time was on the Holy Day itself, the various aunts, uncles and cousins taking it in turn to attract Father's interest elsewhere, while one by one they filed into the kitchen complete with open hand and empty tea-cup. Bessie was not averse to having her hand crossed with silver. I can't remember if there was a Trades Union over this, but everyone seemed happy.

When Father found out what had been going on, he told us how fortunate it was that Bessie should be witness to the broadmindedness of the Protestant clergy. There were, after all quite a number of things about Ireland that were greater than Father.

Bessie's home was a small, whitewashed cottage near Kilkeel. She and her sister shared it, and we think the only reason why elderly Bessie came to work was to get away from the sister. Did I tell you that I took my eldest, Simon, to the cottage not long after Bessie had left Ballymartin, and as soon as we stepped inside we knew that Bessie was a witch? *There* was the black pot hanging on a hook above the fire, with something hissing and popping in it. In one armchair sat Bessie, less hair on head, her nose reaching the chin. The black cat lay curled on the other armchair, and there was no sign of the sister.

'The Divil it is. 'Tis Simon!' She ignored me, because being the good Catholic witch she was, I'd been dismissed for the first in the family to be divorced. She had liked my former husband Michael and had recognized a charmer when she saw one, and allowed herself to be taken in by all the flattery. But, as you know, Peggy, I'm not prejudiced. Bessie didn't exactly take the broomstick to the cat, but she threw something else at it, so Simon and I were sitting on either side of the fireplace, Bessie stirring and stirring.

'Where's the sister?' Simon whispered as we both tried to see into the black pot.

She'd been to London once, had Bessie, and, surprisingly, had seen the ballet. When the moon was full, or she'd a drop or two taken, she would give us a demonstration in the kitchen of what girls did with their feet and legs, her long grey skirt hitched up to her knees. She dismissed the male dancers with their tight unseemly trousers.

'Bessie wasn't born,' you said. 'She was invented. She's a product of Ireland, emerging from the rocks and the soil and the mystical creative aura of the place.'

You danced with her and loved it. She was nearer to you than to us, and as her right toe touched the floor, and yours was doing likewise, she had the smile of the *corps de ballet* floating across the time stage of theatres. She was, of course, at one with nature, particularly the animal kingdom. As fast as Mother would set traps for the mice and rats, Bessie would release them. The outside larder was a kaleidoscoping mixture of buzzing flies, saucers of food, sprung traps, plates of herrings, nibbled bits of cheese, little messages that had significance for Bessie, and, if we were lucky, the large leg of lamb for Sunday lunch.

Did you remember that Father, the youngest of the seven boys, was made to do the carving, and, before he could get started on his own plate, the eldest were up for second helpings?

At night after we had all gone to bed, Bessie would put out saucers of milk for the little people who only appeared in the dark. In the morning the milk had gone. Wandering goats and sometimes donkeys knew where to come. Although I have resisted the temptation to believe in all the whimsicality of the little people, I remember your words:

'If the little people did show, they'd have come

down from the mountains and would be tough as hell, like all mountain people. They'd not be trotting along with the turf-cutter's donkey looking quaint and adorable and full of Blarney-stone-like smiles.' I remember studying you at the time, looking at the small neatness of you and wondering how you knew so much about the little people.

I'm not sure if I ever told you about the time I took younger son Nick and Mike's boy, Rhoderick, to stay at Killowen cottage, the sidekick to the bigger house. The three of us were on our own, and when Nick and Rhoderick went to Dublin for forty-eight hours, and I was alone, the melancholia that is behind a lot of the laughter and the drinking in Ireland, took hold of me. Eire, straight across Strangford Loch, looked threatening, and Finn McCool on his mountain showed me an unfriendly face. The marine gunboat which patrols the loch, protecting the citizens on either side from each other, had disappeared. It was my first and last time of feeling a foreigner in this beautiful land. But I thought of Margaret and Gerald in the house up the lane and their year-in and year-out vigil – Gerald going round the garden at night with dog, torch and gun – a slowly moving target. If they can stand it for the whole of their life, I can on a two-week visit. Fear would simply make the IRA feel at home. Today, because of their actions, and because of the actions of the so-called Loyalists, they are the strangers. Abuse of one's own country and countryfolk turns the perpetrator into an outcast.

Because of the remoteness of this property at

Killowen, Gerald sleeps with an electric button by his bed. Should there be an attack he'd press the button, which would send up a flare from the roof, alerting the gunboat, the gunboat contacting the Security Forces by wire, and Security would be down within ten minutes. What does *within* mean? It doesn't take long to cut through barbed wire, silence the dog with a kick, fire through the lock and enter the house machine-gunning every room. Mind you, Peggy, Sarah has been waiting for them. She's not only cooking for Gerald and Margaret, she's protecting them. She's got arms stashed under the bed, so she says. When I was leaving Killowen last time, Sarah suddenly handed me a mug, Union Jack on one side, and, on the reverse Ulster says no: I'm not sure exactly to what, but to almost anything that has ever been suggested.

I wouldn't envy the IRA facing the wrath of Sarah. It has been building up for seventy-four, and over this she isn't joking. She's joking quite a lot of the time, but you mightn't know it. She tried it on: 'The Mistress wants rid of me, and two wee girls will come in my place. The Major would like that.' 'Don't be ridiculous, Sarah, they couldn't do without you.' Nor could they, but Sarah likes to hear it said.

The visit to Dublin had fired up Nick's and Rhoderick's appetite for a bit of grown-up fun. They took a bus to Ballymartin with a satchel full of food. Nick, already a big boy of sixteen with defensive shoulders, and Rhoderick, slightly older, smaller, were a fine pair as they set out on another adventure. A diving competition off the Black Rock got the energy going and this led to a visit to the Rogers where they were invited to tea. There being two daughters home from university, the chat got better and the tea invitation extended to become an invitation to a dance later in the Orange Hall. There not being a telephone in the Rogers house, Nick and Rhoderick – with the fear I'd say no – put telephoning out of their minds. Into them came all the joy and laughter of a good Catholic family entering an Orange Hall, dressed up to the nines, Nick and Rhoderick full of the good strong tea by then, topped up by glasses of what they thought was only stout, their English reserve flying out of the window. It was only when they returned to me – driven there by an older Rogers son – and noisily coming through the door, that they realized things were not quite right.

Nick's mother was fiercely pushing the Hoover up and down the carpets, her blood pressure making fierce red splodges all over her face, imagining every sort of terrorist action they could come up against out there in the dark night.

'Where the hell have you been?' I screamed at them.

'Uh . . . we . . .'

'Yes?'

'. . . were invited to a dance.'

'A dance was it? Do you know what the time is?'

'No.'

'It's three o'clock in the morning.'

Well, Peggy, do you know what they did? They threw back their heads and laughed – fit to burst, the fumes of alcohol coming out of their mouths, their ears, the pores of their skin. I got them to bed eventually, saying they'd hear more from me in the morning, and while they slept the sleep of the innocent, I tossed and turned, trying to bring down the blood pressure.

I don't believe our cousin Margaret has ever had a duster in her hand. Why should she? She has a brain, and uses it. The Law Society gave a big dinner for her on her eightieth birthday. She's a senior citizen of the best. Loyal, single-minded, intolerant of pettiness, and simply loves to spend – probably quite a lot of – money on clothes. Otherwise she's fairly frugal. We have talks about clothes. We were actually discussing whether a particular shade of lipstick would go with her new suit from Dublin when the bomb at the border near Newry, which killed a judge and his wife, went off, exploding with an evil thud. The lipstick was put back in its case and into the drawer, the suit was hung up, and then she turned to me: 'Will you and Peggy still want to go on the trip to Armagh?'

Gerald came into the room: 'We'll take a different route.' He would be driving us to visit the beautiful city of Armagh, set on a hill, and with its two cathedrals, one Protestant, the other Catholic.

Do you remember, Peggy, choosing carefully what to wear that morning? You thought blue was suitable for eternity, and I went for yellow, for the sun, a defiance of blackness and death.

We set forth and heard on the radio who had been killed. We drove in silence at first, then eighty-five-year-old Gerald said: 'The police at the barriers will have something to say about the Major setting forth with *two* "wumen".' We came to a crossroads, with you pointing: 'Crossmaglen two miles,' it said.

When we stopped just short of the climb to Armagh to have lunch in an inn, I said to you in a whisper: 'I'm going to look under the car when we come out.'

'Don't you talk in there, your English accent is too marked,' said you. 'Marked' seemed a suitable word.

Inside was a white-skinned, dark-haired, blue-eyed couple who never took their eyes off us. They followed us into the dining-room and spoke to each other in soft caressing voices.

I looked under the car when we came out and Gerald asked if I'd lost anything.

The journey back through lush and dangerous Armagh was interrupted by the sight of a mound of flowers on either side of the road. If you remember, Peggy, it was where the nun had been killed, and these flowers were acting as some sort of negation of the horrible deed.

One of the difficult aspects of being in a country that is in a perpetual state of emergency is the disbelief that anything can happen to you when you are on familiar ground. Not here! Not here! you keep saying to yourself, and then one day it happens. It happened for me when I was sitting alone on the

Black Rock — you had not yet returned to Ulster — when the sound of a revving engine caused me to look up to the road. Any army convoy was going past, and in the last open Land Rover were six members of the Parachute Regiment, all with guns pointing outwards, but for the moment the light-hearted banter hid the reality. I left the Black Rock — the mood had been altered — and followed on down the road after them in my small hired car. Twenty minutes on from there I heard the terrible, and all too familiar, thud of death. I drove slowly, my head partly out of the window, and was stopped by a barricade that was suddenly there.

'What is it?' I yelled, and the two policemen called out: 'It's the Paras. The bastards have got them.'

It was the terrible killing outside Warrenpoint. The large haycart on the side of the road hid the weapon of destruction, which the wheels of the Land Rover had detonated as they went over the wire on the road. Most were killed outright, the remaining two, concussed and confused, started shooting in all directions, and an English visitor, on the other side of the water, taking a walk in Eire, got a bullet through his heart.

I drove on the short distance to Killowen, to find both Margaret and Sarah on the doorstep, white-faced.

'Thank God,' they both said.

'They've got Mountbatten on his boat off the harbour of Mullaghmore in County Sligo.' Gerald had come out from the sitting-room.

Gerald has never had – and never will have – anything good to say about the Republican movement. He has trained his mind to listen only to news about loyalist Ulster, which to him means Protestant Ulster. He sees the IRA as a target for his gun, should they come near. He is not afraid. His life, he feels, has not got much more spool in it, so he might as well take a few members of the IRA when he goes.

His very vocal views became known, and perhaps only he was surprised when, a few years back, members of the SAS came without warning to protect him from his well-known attitude. He could hardly accept the indignity of the British Army sending men in to silence him from his personal battle. But on the day his office was targeted and successfully bombed, and the SAS had stopped him from going in to Newry, he understood, at last, that they knew their business.

A white tradesmen's van had, mysteriously, got through his locked gate and barbed wire, and out of it had strode a tall, erect young man, asking for Gerald. He had shown Gerald his SAS badge and announced that for the next three weeks six of his men would be protecting him. The officer left and the men stayed, always two of them with Gerald, two others asleep, and the remaining two hidden in the garden. Gerald was not allowed to go anywhere in his car; he travelled instead in varying coloured vans, which, in turn arrived every few days with the NAAFI rations.

Sarah enjoyed every minute of their stay, exchanging Irish wit for cockney, and helped them with the cooking of their rations which was done in one of the garages. The SAS enjoyed Sarah, the toughness of her, and her absolute opinions.

It was only at the end of their visit, when the young officers returned that Gerald learned that at the time of their arrival the Major had been number one on the hit list.

Would you believe, Peggy, that a few years later, when I was staying with friends in Wiltshire, this particular officer from the SAS came as a guest to lunch. I had been warned not to ask him about his career. From the moment he stepped in through the door I had the queerest feeling that he'd been around County Down a time or two.

'I gather you're in the army,' said I. 'Has it ever taken you to Northern Ireland?' The family were out of earshot.

'Oh yes.'

Oh yes indeed.

'My father came from there. I return every year,' I said.

'What part?'

'*Where the mountains of Mourne sweep down to the sea,*' I hummed. 'You wouldn't know it, it's a small place between Newry and Kilkeel.'

'Killowen', he said, and smiled broadly – I was proud to guess that I looked a little like my cousin Margaret.

'The Major's a tough one,' he continued. 'We admired him.'

'Coincidences are a fine thing.'

'Yes, a fine thing.'

We joined in the general conversation, knowing that no names had been said and that it was in both our interests to keep quiet.

That evening of Mountbatten's murder Gerald and Margaret were due to give a dinner party for me, with most of the relations. Some were coming up from the South, others down from Belfast, some locally. It did not occur to either Margaret or Gerald to cancel it. Sarah, who was already in her black maid's dress with small lace apron, said the meal was already under way and the meat would spoil. 'Them's not worth cancelling anything for.'

Best dress on, suits out of the press, the family came. They came on the high road, they came on the low road, they came over mountain and through valley, and no one, not one, Peggy, was late. You'd have been proud of the Fishers then, and the McKibbens and the Annetts, and however many other connections that go to make up the word *family*. It has to be said that King Billie left a little bit more behind than just the sickening Orange Order.

It takes a lot to equal an Irish funeral, the ground soaked from the crying, the town turning out to follow the coffin, and members of the family openly tearful, heads bent, being supported, and walking immediately behind the coffin. Today, in Ulster, soldiers line the route, the priest in flowing robes saying the words that will bring comfort to the bereaved. The bent sad heads have little to do with the wake that is to follow: 'For God's sake, Maureen, he's better out of it.'

The not-so-long-ago poverty of the Catholic underclasses was increased because of the money saved for the coffin. It's nothing new. I've seen the never-to-be-forgotten Egyptian pyramids of death. The pyramids in Mexico are smaller, more intimate. Even more memorable are the recently excavated Minoan Funerary Palaces in Crete. Perhaps living was the better deal there.

Did you know that Michael commanded the Airborne Brigade for some years? Although I left him in the end, I never felt I was leaving the Paras. I think I should say a word for the Paras and the condemnation of them in Londonderry. Tough men – some recruited from the prisons, having to exercise control in their heavy hot army gear while young boys – seeing it as a game – hurling rocks and stones at them, the soldiers expected to remain steadfast for the whole of their tour of duty, and, perhaps, occasionally, breaking out from orders. Perhaps not. Perhaps sometimes it was the orders that were wrong.

It's every sort of tragedy the killing at Warrenpoint, and for me my Irish sense of hospitality was shattered that such a thing could happen, on familiar ground, to my mother's kinsmen. Anger is about the only feeling left after such an attack, and disgust, and, of course it is anger that can turn to revenge. Turn the other cheek? Not likely, and that's how the

Loyalist Freedom Fighters have illustrated the point.

Dear, dear cousin, you have been asked if you would like a visit from a Macmillan nurse. You know what Macmillan nurses are. They come to give moral support. The one that was sent from the Marsden Hospital annoyed you so much that you felt *she* was the one needing help. How like you to have carried your professionalism on into your illness. Preparing the way for others has, in a sense, been your mission. Not that God has featured – as a subject – between us, more for me than for you because we had Him living with us at the Manse. We had to sing grace to the Almighty before and after meals. And in the morning the household gathered for prayers in Father's study, Oats scratching at the door. If Father was late the scratching became thumps. This was Oats's time for a walk out onto the glebe with Father – Father saying 'Rabbits!' and Oats off like a rocket to rabbit hill.

Today Father would have been open-minded about the theories of Hawkins and Dawkins, though less so Dawkins who, I believe, does not really permit of a deity. Discussion about the Big Bang or belief in a universe without a beginning or end would also have been permitted. In those days my irritating and constant 'But why?' was met with 'That's the mystery'. And reference to the fact that if even Isaac Newton bowed before it, so could I.

But on the whole Father liked questions. He died asking one.

'Marjorie,' he called out to Mother, 'I've always been meaning to ask you . . .'

'Yes?'

Silence. A heart attack took him away. What was his question – 'Was it a strain on you being the wife of a clergyman?' Or 'Was your world of music an alternative to a closeness with me?' Or 'Do you still have Faith?'

Did she ever?

Mother's answer might have been in the form of a question: 'Was I ever enough of a companion to *you*?'

It can't have been easy for her when she first came to Scotland. Can you imagine it? The countryside was beautiful around, but the nearest house a mile away and the village further. For company, when Father was reorganizing Southern Scotland, who had she? Broad-Scots-speaking maids, their tongue as foreign as German – and not so dissimilar. It must have been then, when she realized she was surrounded by a lot of – what her mother insisted on calling – foreigners, that Mother went inwards. I only hope that whatever was going on in her private world made her a little bit happy. And, of course, she had her music, and her garden.

Father's death left a vacuum. He was the inspiration for us all. He was behind Mike getting that very good scholarship to his public school. He was the inspiration for my passing into the Ambulance Corps, as a driver of those huge box ambulances, towards the end of the war. He was the inspiration behind all of Oats's acts of defiance, because they were both from Ireland and understood about rebels.

Father never wrote down any of his sermons. They were all in the mind, the best filing system he ever had. But there was a woman who sang in the choir at Crossmichael Church, Mrs Carruthers – she'd been there as long as Father – and for those forty-four years she wrote down the text for every sermon. If Father ever repeated one, Mrs Carruthers' head would turn and she would look up at the pulpit: Don't you dare.

On Burns Night most of Scotland went out to revere the haggis. An emblem of Robbie Burns, I suppose. Father, who never quite lost his Irish intonation, was invited year after year to give the Burns address at whatever dinner he was attending. Peggy, I hope it is not boastful to say I never heard a better speaker – out of the pulpit, I mean. Mother would sit, mostly with her eyes shut, and towards the end of the speech praying that she was going to understand the joke when it came. For most people in the audience it was no problem because at the penultimate stage of the speech Father's shoulders would begin to shake, then his stomach, and finally he could hardly get the words out because of the laughter. Following the address there were some poems to be read, by Father. It's difficult enough to imagine the translation of broad Scots into Russian – the Russian a lover of this working man's poet – but to understand how the Scots could listen to Burns through the tones of Ulster you have got to understand that the Scots loved Father.

Words, words, Father was great with them, each one encouraging the next, imagination taking flight as he went along. And in the pulpit, at the beautiful passages from the Bible, the tears falling down his face. Pain and suffering did not make Father cry. Beauty did.

What was in the house at Ballymartin for us to play with, other than the inherited imagination? There was, one must admit, an old spinning-wheel in the long sitting-room, a pack of cards that was in a drawer in a table just inside the door, and there were the shells, of varying sizes and colour, lined up just inside the fender. When you listened to the shells, pressed close to the ear, the sea came into the room. According to the day – damp, hot, windy, wet – the shells gave out different sounds. So, if punishment was around and we'd been forbidden the shore, we'd pick up a shell.

No. There were no toys, and people coming to see us never brought any. The only time I was given a doll I cut off its bright red hair, blackened its face and took it for a walk in my doll's pram which was kept for walking the kittens. Perhaps Mike is right, I really did want to be a boy. Mind you, getting down the drive at the Manse with my pram full of kittens without bird shit dropping all over us wasn't easy. We had a fine rookery, high up in our stately beech trees, the branches fanning out at the top and the nests balancing there against the wind. Beech trees, the lightest of green in the spring, the colour gradually moving through rich summer to the muted shades of autumn, colours I've copied in every sitting-room I've decorated. The rooks remained in command, Father forbidding farmers coming to take a pot shot at them. So they shat over the drive, and Jessie, the woman who came to wash sheets in our wash-house, letting the mess from her hair get to the clean linen.

Jessie's mind was nearly as dirty as Annie's. When they were together the house shook. Coming from the back regions of the Manse were noises that some of the visiting parishioners found a little out of place. They could tell you a thing or two, those maids, and if you, Peggy had been found in the summer house displaying your private parts by one of them, you'd have stood up to your Mother even more, because your knowledge would have been greater than hers.

Down on the shore at Ballymartin there certainly was no need for toys. Nature provided them. There was the wet sand for the building of castles which Oats could destroy, there was the hard dry sand for cricket – the beginning of Mike's lifelong passion – and then there were the stones. The coast in parts of Ulster is full of volcanic rock and very ancient stone, about 50 million years of it, and with the cooling of the lava – over several ice ages – the Mourne Mountains were formed. The smooth oblong-shaped stones became our racing cars, the variety of shapes were every bit as good as the variety on the market. As we went to the TT car races at Newtownards every year, we knew about the sounds of racing cars, as we did the names of the men who raced in them.

Our parents would be sitting further along the shore, away from the noise of roaring engines, horns, police sirens – a magnificent stream of sound coming out of our mouths; sounds that managed to deaden their complaints that we were disturbing the quiet and the beauty of the landscape.

We were told that before man used the stone, he worshipped it. So perhaps that is why – when we were older – we hid our stones somewhere in the bankhead. We had thought of building a cairn like the megalithic tomb on Slieve Donard, but knew it would be destroyed. We even fantasized that the buried ones might turn up like the Dead Sea Scrolls, to be found centuries hence with our scribblings on them. You were the one to write on the stones, along with your own hieroglyphics, and if they are ever to be found there will be a laugh in it.

It was you, also, that underlined the union between the four of us. It was you that gave meaning to loyalty and a sense of belonging in its abstract form. I don't think you knew fully what you were doing, but today I see instinct in it. When people talk about the *otherness* of Man, I see the paradox of you, the Peggy of reality that has done with euphemisms; and then I see the Peggy that knows that the Little People, who can sometimes be big, are in real Irish terms, *the fairies*. It wasn't only Bessie who had a closeness to animals, you, with your Egyptian cats, would look with your deep fathoming eyes into their slanting luminous ones and who knows what understanding there was.

'The Macmillan nurse is here again.' I don't think she's ever been away.

Your eyes are opening: 'Tell her she's an interfering nuisance.'

'She's in the room, Peggy.'

'Tell her to get out. Besides, I want a cigarette.'

'If it's anger that's going to bring you back to us, I'll keep her here.'

The nurse says: 'The nice vicar of St Mary's has suggested that you might like a little church counselling.'

You heave yourself up: 'I'll do my own counselling.' You speak with a big voice. Pride talking.

'But the vicar would give you the message from God.'

'Do you know nothing at all?' says Irish Peggy. 'God and psychotherapists have a lot in common. They both go for the jugular.'

I can see that it's working, because there is a reluctant smile on your face, and the Macmillan nurse is amused. She's reluctant to go. It's not every day she meets a fully-trained doctor, fully-trained analyst, terminally ill in bed and articulating. She creeps out of the room as she sees you sink down into the bed.

I think of those who say we have the same smile — broad, welcoming. It lights up the face, they say. Thank God we never went in for face-lifts. All those little creases and wrinkles round the eyes would have gone, personality annihilated.

It's not a secret any more that following the birth of your son, John, and the rejection by your mother of his existence, you had the double task of giving your brains an extra polish to earn a good living, and to look after your child. For some of the relations in Ulster, for whom fabrication was a better bet than exposure – not so unusual after the war – we concocted a story that your greatest friend and her husband had been killed in a car crash, and you had adopted their son. You became his guardian. As it happened John came into the world with a mass of red golden hair and no apparent facial resemblance to you, except, perhaps, the colour of his eyes. The guardian idea held good until two of our more discerning cousins came out with the question: 'Is John yours?'

'Uh . . . Yes.'

So, there it was. The lie exploded, and you feeling a lot better for it, but it took you another thirty years to get you back to Ulster. And then because I took you.

During your wilderness years your life became two-dimensional: work and John. You were always rushing from one to another, and when your clinic for mothers and children proved free of challenge you added a third dimension – analysis – and having accepted the large part psychiatry plays in all medicine, you went for full analysis yourself – seven years in all – in order to qualify.

But your mother's repudiation had nearly turned the electric Peggy into a seriously grinding little cog in the wheel of life. Until ... you saw what was happening to you and said to yourself: So what! I've got a son, I've got independence, and the sun shines nearly every day.

So it was back to the laughter, and to the marriage to stable ex-Navy Commander, Peter, and the giving of a life to John and the watching him grow into a very nice man with your and Warren's brain, and – I'm reluctant to accord the praise – his father's satirical wit. Not bad for a little sperm who nearly never was.

'Robert,' you say, 'has he been?'

'I think you'd know.'

It's fair to add, just for the record – of the family scrapbook – that the latter days of your pregnancy, when Society decreed that you hide away, you came to us in the Manse of Crossmichael. The 'No, I won't' part of you was reborn with the birth of John, when, following the agreement to have the baby adopted – because how could you cope? – and the nursing home prescribing that you never see the baby, you announced to those in attendance:

'I want to see him.'

The nurse who was walking away with her arms full of afterbirth and baby, turned round. So, John had a second birth when he came into your arms.

The early years of marriage are exclusive to everything but itself. For you it was life in London, living with a retired naval officer whose two main interests were music and Egyptian cats. Pleasantly passive. For me it was life around the globe with an active army officer whose two main interests were the army and his career. Stimulating, but singular.

We kept in touch, sometimes on hot wires over cool water, and increasingly so as the years went on.

By the time Michael was commanding the Airborne Battalion and we were stationed in Aldershot, I, as the CO's wife, had to visit some of the houses of the 'other ranks' when one of them had taken to stealing. 'Go and find out what's going on,' was Michael's injunction. Now, as it happens, Peggy, I am a great believer in minding my own business as opposed to someone else's. I had learnt from my father that sitting at home with the door open is a better incentive to communication than visiting people in their houses when not invited. So, when I had to find one of the houses in the army barracks, knock on the door, and *if* it was opened, announce my business – which was her business – and wait to have the door shut in my face, I knew I was acting contrary to my own beliefs.

The door opened, and the woman wearing comfortable-looking bedroom slippers, her manner relaxed and a cigarette hanging from her mouth, invited me into the kitchen and told me to get on with what I had come to say.

Against a background of a new type of washing-machine that jumped and gurgled and sploshed water on the floor, a radio blaring on the table, and a television flashing lights in the corner, I attempted discussion about their circumstances.

I knew already what were the circumstances, and as I was seen through the door, I understood why the Para was stealing. Nothing, ever, would be enough for this woman, and to keep her in comfortable bedroom slippers and all the latest in gadgets, this Para, who'd been with Michael in some of the more tricky parts of the world, was reduced to finding money on the other side of the law.

'Don't put him in prison,' I said to Michael, 'just post him somewhere where wives can't follow.'

Now if you think I was running the brigade, let me tell you that the Paras know their good officers when they see them.

I have a fairly large thank-you to deliver to the army for my free visit to Kenya, Cyprus, America, Mexico. I wouldn't unhappen any of it because, as we know, the only brain that is expanding in the whole of the kingdom of man and animal is man's. A visit here and a visit there, and the abundance of curiosity that goes with it, builds on that brain a fraction by adding to the bank of knowledge and sensation.

Swimming on the latitude of the Equator in a pool of syrup-like velvet, as we looked through a tropical forest to the high snow-capped summit of Mount Kilimanjaro, was the apex of my sensuous journey through Africa.

But the deep, deep pool of our own swimming in 'the gulf' area of the Black Rock is at the sharp end of that particular sensation.

Do you realize that we swam in the sea at Ballymartin several times a day? We swam and dried, and played with stones, and we swam and dried and played cricket, we swam and dried and rushed up the bank head, into the dining-room, feet bare, and ate with full concentration Mary's mounds of pancakes, and before the last mouthful was munched, we were across the road and down again, knowing that there'd be a telling-off later.

You might like it if I paint a word-picture of the shore, but first I must tell you about the sea on calm August days. There were about three shades, leading from the dry sand outwards. The nearest sands were a pale brown sugar, getting browner as the sea pulled; the sea a translucent turquoise while the water was still over the sand, and then, as the great waves came, the water taking into itself shades of aquamarine, and finally to ink black. I remember once sitting a little way off from one of our games, and wondering if I'd ever be able to reproduce what I saw in paint.

As you know, I wasn't. Aged thirty, already the wife of a battalion commanding colonel, and a mother, I went from Aldershot to an art school, dressed – I hoped – like every other student: jeans, smocks, sandals, and was lucky enough to have as art teacher Mr Cheesman. From him came the *microscopic* understanding of the beauties of nature, even in to mud. All his paintings were of the earth, realized. Dark, succulent, welcoming. These artists illustrate that we should look beneath our feet.

Just after Michael had been posted to Kenya – wife and children to follow later – as GI Ops (I never discovered what G stood for) to the new general commanding East Africa, I said good-bye to Mr Cheesman with regret, and he said: 'Don't try to paint views when you're in Africa. Africa is too big a canvas. Try for something smaller, like the people.' I became so magnetically drawn to the huge sweep that I broke my heart trying to do just that. So, replacing the paintbrush with the pen, I wrote in a fever for fear of losing it all. At first Michael was indifferent to my preoccupation, but when I went deeper into the 'meaning of life' – which should be got over during student years – like studying the philosophy of some Indian mystic, he said 'I'd rather you brought a lover into this house than have the place overcrowded by this self-styled mystic.'

OK.

But I didn't take a lover. I found a friend. I joined the local sketch group, and was attracted to a man who painted large abstracts. It seemed curious in such a setting, but soon I understood that nature was its own canvas in areas such as the great Rift Valley. Val had little sense of either place or of possession. He lived in an office that belonged to some firm during the day, and in the evening he turned it into his strangely vibrant room. He didn't appear to have money, and existed on a diet of local fruit and the delicious home-grown tea. He was without ambition, so in the end his large, strangely dignified paintings hung in the Indian solicitor's office. The solicitor didn't attempt to explain them to his clients, but instead just hoped that their problems might be diminished by the deeply felt expressions round the walls.

Val was one of the few contemporary artists – and I am prepared to call him that – who was generous about other modern painters.

When I wrote to you about him, you wrote back: 'If he's free of the tyranny of possessions, make the most of his ideas.'

I did.

The Military Headquarters in Nairobi was highly operational because the War Minister in London had told the General Officer Commanding to 'get out there and bring in those Mau Mau from the forests, or else.' The previous General Officer Commanding the military in East Africa had failed to do so. On the morning of his departure from Kenya the East African Standard had a blank sheet for its front page, and printed at the bottom was: 'That which was achieved by General Erskine while serving here.'

Cruel? Yes. But we were at war.

It was difficult sometimes to equate war conditions with the hobby of *our* General. He'd been chosen for the job because he was well known to be a good chooser of subordinates, which meant that he had self-interested powers of delegation. He was an avid birdwatcher, and having found for himself a real Mr Fixit as a Military Assistant, general dogsbody, a reconnaissance would be arranged into a forest that held both the Mau Mau and the wonderful birds of

Kenya. Headquarters would be happy for at least five days while the General was out of their way, combat dress on, field-glasses to his eyes, small edition of *Birds of East Africa* in his tunic pocket.

Michael's and my first visit to the matchless Serengeti was with the General and his wife, Jean. We did it in comfort, nearly spoiling us for rougher safaris. There was a soldier servant, soldier chef, and game ranger. Eating out at night round the campfire we were treated to a profusion of sound, often the hyena imitating other animals, and all combining to produce the effect of Mahler in full orchestra. Conversation ceasing, we heard chord and discord, the high flute of the night-time birds, the sighs of the smaller animals, the trombone snores of the bigger ones, and the incessant click of the cicadas. The only aspect that reminded us of why we were in this God-inspired country, was the stamping of the soldiers' feet every time the General spoke to them. 'Stand at ease' wouldn't have made any difference because they saw themselves as being in a country at war and they were there to protect the General. This time from the wild animals. The Mau Mau did not penetrate into the very open bushland.

Daylight at 5 a.m. saw us into the Land Rovers, revving our way through roadless bush, once more in search of the bushland birds. No one, not the Governor, nor the Chief of Police, nor a visiting dignitary, was allowed to put foot to ground when on safari. As far as our General was concerned, that rule was for the rest of the world. So climb down he did and almost immediately disappeared among some thorn trees. Michael stood erect, viewing the landscape through field-glasses. Spotting a general was not what he'd come to Kenya to do, unless, of course, it was a self-styled general in the Mau Mau.

One ton of rhino hitting the Land Rover at our combined speed would have made lunch for the vultures, but the General's wife already had the animal in her sights with the camera, and gave the command.

'Move quickly. To the right. Now to the left. No. No. Wait a minute.' That minute nearly did for us as she clicked and clicked again. But the rhino's charge is always straight, its little unrevolving eyes take it into a run from which it cannot be diverted. The explosion of dust, the roar, the smell that accompanies one ton of animal flesh passing your flank, leaves the impression that you have, actually, been hit.

You and Peter, with an opaque home life, were galvanized when travelling, he scratching the ground for the mosaics of antiquity, and you in the bazaars buying more, ever more, colourful material, curiosity the motivating force for every ancient discovery.

But it was on your last trip, to India, when you were returning in the aircraft that you understood you were losing your ten-year fight with cancer.

Yes, you've woken up. The word is in your brain, in your waking, in your sleeping. And because you are a worldly, intelligent, understanding psychiatrist of a woman, you have not denied the actual name of the illness. You have spoken it aloud. You've even tried to personalize it. Talking to your left breast as it gives another dart of pain: 'Stop it', you say, identifying with the breast and punishing the enemy. But yesterday they found a different drug for you, and today you are philosophical.

'Did I tell you,' say you, lapsing further into the Irish brogue, 'what one of my patients said to me before I came into this dump?'

'What did she say?'

'Dr Fry, whatever happens to you, I want you to know that you're actually in my head, a welcome presence forever.'

'It's your immortality.'

You grin.

Encouraged by the tone of the conversation, I chance: 'Do you think we might all be molecules inside some cosmic arterial system . . . full of its own intent?'

'Not now, Pauline.'

'Oh Peggy!'

I sit back in the chair.

We've been together on the visit to Ulster for the last eight years. We've tried to avoid the days of 'celebration' – drums, pipes, bowler hats, banners, solemn unyielding faces – and we have discovered new – old – favourite places. For instance there's the Silent Valley – oh what a name! Birdsong is rare on these volcanic giants, free almost of bush and tree except, lower down, the tenacious and delicious bilberry; the shadows of the mountains, purple, pink, mauve, creating their own vision of strength and very ancient beauty.

The motto of the boarding school I went to in England was 'Quietness and Strength.' I couldn't see the point of it then, but I have since, and, in a way, I sense it in this room – in spite of the talker you once were, and still, sometimes, are.

The point about the Silent Valley, is that once you're fully into it, and look up at the various verticals around, you begin to talk in whispers, because, as with the African interior, you're not quite sure if you have a place in it. Today army patrol vehicles go up and down the valley because of the great dam at the top. The IRA could – and I am sure still would – like to disrupt the lives of thousands by getting their murderous explosives into it.

The first time we saw a military Land Rover appearing from out of one of the mountains, passing us on our silent walk and disappearing again into one of those blue-pink shadows, we wondered if some distant beam of ill intent had reached our minds. By the time yet another year had gone by, and another, we had come to expect these – strangely silent – protectors.

The little café snugged against the foot of one of the mountains – Binian I think – became one of our chatting havens. Here is the centre of the Ulster we have known and loved. In order to get to the area, you drive, ride, or walk out of Kilkeel, up a narrow road that gets narrower, surrounded by little square fields bordered by either hedges or walls. Dikes we call them. It was on that last drift up the little mountain road that you said: 'Stop the car.' You got out, turned, looked towards the sea, and said: 'I wonder if I'll be back.'

Then, walking swiftly towards the car, you said: 'It's a strong cup of tea we need.'

No matter what time of the day you visit the café in the Market Square in Kilkeel you get: 'Sure it's great to see yous back again', and this even if you've been in the day before. 'What'll you have?' from the little girl waitress already writing down large pot of tea for two and fresh soda bread.

'It's a grand day, isn't it just,' from the waitress who is back with a heavy black tray, sliding cups and saucers onto the table, and, at the same time, removing the ashtray.

'That will do you no good at all with all the good mountain air to cure you.'

How did she know?

'Bring that back', from you, tucking into the soda bread and pointing at the ashtray. But the little girl waitress, with her hair a frizz round her face, was soon holding one of your hands and telling you that you had helped her Auntie over there in London.

'In London, so you did.'

'Quinns the butcher,' you said with delight, 'the best sausages either side of the water.' And then: 'Is your Auntie better now?' as the wee girl nodded, and you stretching for your cigarettes, the room full of the smoke of them. We had guessed then, and certainly know now, that the cigarettes would kill you. Lung cancer is the most recent of your cancers diagnosed.

At the time you telephoned me from your house in Richmond: 'I don't want you to say: "I told you so", but the X-rays show fairly massive cancer of the lung.'

Actually, dear, dear Peggy, I told you so a long time ago. The telephone call just made me weep.

The Marines' boat that can be seen from the garden of cousin Margaret's house through a gap in a high hedge is difficult to photograph, because it doesn't take long for it to pass the gap. But your determination to have it on record had you standing there for some time. It's known now as 'Peggy's boat', and I'm sure the Marines would be pleased. At one point they couldn't come ashore. They tried it for a time.

'A packet of State Express please,' to the shop-keeper in Rostrevor.

Silence. And no movement.

'Oh well then, I'll get them somewhere else.'

'Indeed you will not.'

It wasn't that they were outright denied dinner in one of the two hotels: they had dinner, but a few days later a bomb got the hotel.

The young soldiers who were sent to Northern Ireland had never witnessed hatred such as that experienced in Ulster. The main targets were, of course, the pure English soldiers sent over to help with the policing.

A long time ago the English obeyed a command

to conquer and slay if necessary. Their descendants mostly don't know about it, or don't care, but they are still having to take the rap in that the Irish Republican Army can weed them out.

'It was the Irish who first civilized the Scots,' say you, 'and then the English,' but I'm wondering in what terms you're using the word 'civilized'.

Mind you, Peggy, I may be treading on difficult ground here; some of the people of the Ulster Plantation were ethnically of the same stock as the Irish at a much earlier date: ancient Pictish-Celtic origin.

And if you want to hear more – it was the Protestantism of these Plantation people that was to become the badge of allegiance to the English Crown. Ulster salutes the Crown, not the English. So, we're back to Symbols, and their significance.

You've opened your eyes, and the sea blue-green of them is raging a bit. Perhaps you don't want symbols; they come into your consulting room in the form of dreams.

As an analyst, Peggy, you know all about the danger of suppressed rage, and when it's also mixed with guilt it becomes the body's destroyer. Unsuppressed rage is what I feel for you now. Rage: rage against the dying of the light. But we don't know if the light is dying for you. I wonder when I look at those shut eyelids what you are seeing, because your mouth – with the little lines upwards at the corners – tell of happy recall.

'If that Macmillan nurse comes again,' you say

81

suddenly, 'tell her to get out. She keeps asking me about my feelings. And I'm not going to share them with her.'

'Oh, well done, Peggy. Let's have more.'

'Was it you that put me into this South American dump?'

'Have you been to South America?'

'Everyone knows what dumps there are in South America.'

Queen Peggy, like Queen Elizabeth I you are. Issuing orders, perhaps even sending your lovers across the globe to smudge large areas of the map with pink and bring you home prizes of priceless worth.

'I'll tell you this, if an Irish rugby team is playing England, the whole of Ireland will be rooting for the Irish, and to hell with the Crown.'

Claudette, the black nurse who comes from Dublin, is standing in the doorway, listening and grinning. She's been in before and watches the strange mobility of such an ill patient, and listens to the whole structured sentences that seem to come almost out of sleep.

'D'you think it has had an effect on us being the hate object of so many?' I remark – to the room, mainly. And Claudette, looking at me, says: 'Us?'

An American once said to me: 'If it weren't for the Irish charm the English would have killed off all of them a long time ago.'

That's it – the witch's potion, charm. The built-in Blarney Stone of a nation.

'Mind you,' the American continued, 'the English have always been too darned arrogant.'

We aren't any more. We go round begging people to like us, as once did the Americans.

When I say 'we' in this context, I am, I think, associating with the English. It's difficult being a hybrid, particularly when one of the mixtures in the pot is Ulster. Most people go about their daily lives without giving a thought to their inheritance, until, that is, they go abroad: aliens this way. But even that will pass soon, already in Europe. An Ulsterman has only to go across the Irish Sea and there are questions.

But you're asleep. The outburst – which you enjoyed – has exhausted you.

One of the areas in Mourne that we keep to ourselves, Peggy, is that strange house your father built near Cranfield, on the sea. It has a seascape and is looking in at the back door of the mountains. From that spot, they fade away, hump, hump, like the movements of a snake, smaller and smaller. The house was structured as the warm part of isolation. We could sit in what was the remains of the garden, looking seaward, without interruption of shrub or tree, and with the backdrop of mountain we felt ourselves a part of what we were seeing.

'You can't beat it,' we'd say to one another, and then would have uncomfortable thoughts of our return to school. Wales for you, England for me. Scotland for Mike, and Ulster for Warren. What were they doing? Trying to separate us?

Do you remember the fuss about finding a tartan I could wear for the dress uniform of my first boarding-school? The uniform was kilt, silk tussore blouse, Harris tweed jacket, and Harris tweed coat. Almost every girl in the school was Scottish, so they knew a thing or two about tartans; there was no good my turning up in something I had no right to wear. So, a certain amount of turning over of cabinet drawers, and looking up and down family trees, revealed an Irish ancestor who had been called McNeill. You'd expect, and the family did, that I'd look a credit to them all, the kilt swinging, with my tall figure, like the best of them. The snag was – and it's been envy from some – that I have a Sassenach bottom. The kilt drooped. I have only one photograph of myself in the school dress uniform, walking down Prince's Street with your Aunt Marj. The Harris tweed full-length coat is on, tie and shirt visible, also long thick socks up to the knees, felt hat with ribbon, but thank God, no sign of the kilt.

You were not all that interested in getting your cousin into a kilt, but you enjoyed the connection with history. You had no trouble at all in turning McNeill into O'Neill, and who is to say you are wrong? – because the bold spirit of the ancient O'Neills is there inside you, perhaps even in us all. For were not the Earls of Tyrone, the last of two thousand years of Gaelic dynastic clan government, the O'Neills, equal to any reigning Tudor?

I'll tell you something else you can say about the

English race: they and their Spanish enemy were a little late in discovering America. Sailing in their three-masted ocean-going ships with their ingenious rigging and steering gear – which seemed to do more for them than any accurate fifteenth-century plotting – the Irish, be it even by mistake, reached America a thousand years earlier. Columbus can go ahead with his obscene mutilating and murdering, loot the only reason for his voyaging – but he was not, *was not*, there first.

I'm not laughing at you, Peggy, just sharing the joy that you are leaving behind such a legacy of speculation; aspects that leave much for questioning cousins to ponder.

We know that you have insight, and we know that that coupled with your professionalism has made you not only a very good analyst but also an interesting travelling companion, the opinions tumbling out along with the facts.

I was with you in your garden in Richmond one night when you had a patient and her husband to dinner. We'd eaten and drunk. We were relaxed, talking intermittently, and you were on the path, making a point to the patient's husband, when Jan, the patient, spotted you and, surprised, said: 'What are you doing there squatting like a wood sprite?'

Instead of being disturbed, she went on looking and I could tell by the expression on her face, that she liked, and in a way, understood, what she saw. The duality of you, giving further substance to her analysis.

In the last year you have taken on no new patients. You have phased out those who were ready, passed on others to colleagues, and a few have become your friends. Patients in the early stages of analysis were probably the only people to whom you did not come out with the word 'cancer', particularly of the breast. You knew they would not have been able to take it. But now all know, and they have been in, bringing you flowers. They have not said 'thank you' because that might herald finalities. But you know why they have come.

There's a new little bird on the tree outside this window, and I'm watching to see if it's his territory for the night, on this slim branch. There are sparrows in the gravel beneath, fluttering their wings into the dust. Is this bathtime as well as bedtime? Do they clean themselves before sleep, like the cat that goes in for licking its coat, and the dog that circulates? There's no doubt that evening can be sad, representing the end of so much. It's the end of Monday, or Tuesday, or Wednesday, and it's the passing of something that can never return. That, Peggy, is why we thank God for memory.

Have you noticed how in Ireland – both Ulster and the South – God is brought into the conversation most of the time, and if not Him then his Son or the Son's mother? Mind you, the 'Divil' has almost equal status. I was sitting at dinner one night, Peggy, at a party given by my publishers, between an ex-Government minister and a well-known cartoonist.

Religion was suddenly the topic between the three of us, and I believe I had brought it up.

'Talking in Stock Exchange terms,' said the cartoonist, 'I'd say the Devils are doing rather better than the Gods these days.'

'Oh,' said the late Minister for War – a man who really knows how the press can hound – 'I sold my Gods a while back. But have bought them back again.'

I think I met the Devil in one of his incarnations at another publisher's dinner. He was a fellow citizen of Galloway, a writer of some note, particularly about the crusades. He put a new word into my vocabulary by telling me that he wasn't writing, he was practising his art as a warlock. To be more accurate, he once *was* a warlock. He'd killed two schoolboys once by sticking pins into the effigies he'd made of them. I'll catch up with this writer one of these days and find out if I was having my little author's leg pulled.

You, with your training as an analyst – as one might say an honorary member of the inner circle – would have enjoyed talking to this man, leading him on to divulge more of his secret life, holding your own. I'm not saying you know anything about witchcraft, Heaven (this time) forbid, but I am saying that you would not have written him off as a madman.

I'll tell you something else: Bessie had insight. The first time I came over to Ulster with Simon and Nick, and minus Michael, Bessie eyed me for a day or two – I knew she was doing it – and wondered what was coming. She then asked: 'You'll be telling me next that you've left Colonel Forrester.'

You see what I mean? It wasn't really a question.

The actress in Bessie put us all on stage. Each August as we drove out the gates on our way home to Scotland, there was Bessie, tea towel in one hand, large handkerchief in the other, tears cascading down her face. Her heart was fit to break, the cunning old witch, and we responding, handkerchiefs fluttering out the car window. It was from my parents that the cheques came at Christmas.

I think I've told before how years ago – I was probably thirteen – I was taken to see an old *wuman* up in the mountains who was reputedly the most accomplished fortune-teller in Ireland, and she was to give me a picture of my life to be. Well, the older cousins tripped out of the dark cavern of a cottage, happily smiling, while I got a closing up of my hand and ''Tis ruled by fate ye're. I can do nothing for ye.'

It had its effect, and for some years, as you may remember, I drifted, accepting things. But said, eventually: After all she was only an old woman in a cottage; what does she know about anything? The only kind of witch I'll accept for the future is the one, the very little one, that's in myself.

Bessie loved Simon and Nick, and had them rolling across the kitchen with her imitations of people, jokes in the Northern tongue, so that I, confident in her caring of them, took a short trip to Dublin.

When I returned, the boys – particularly Simon, who's always had a good ear – had a new vocabulary in broad Belfast, that was summed up in his greeting when we told him about Dublin and the good restaurants: 'Lucky buggers,' said he.

'Surely to God, the pair of yous, you've more sense than to talk to your Mammy like that.'

I know you said that once the monkey-puzzle fell down from sheer old age, Ballymartin was never quite the same. You may be right – or perhaps it was a turning point. But no, our sense of wonder did not go with it.

If you understand what sense of wonder means, I don't believe you lose it. It is perhaps the most precious gift the baby brings with it. It survives the agony of birth, it defies some of the disillusionments of growing up and, one can hope, it affixes itself to the DNA gene that passes it on. Perhaps Words-worth's poem *Intimations of Immortality* expressed it most lyrically with:

> *Our birth is but a sleep and a forgetting,*
> *The Soul that rises with us, our life's Star*
> *Hath elsewhere its setting,*
> *And cometh from afar;*
> *Not in entire forgetfulness,*
> *And not in utter nakedness*
> *But trailing clouds of glory do we come*
> *From God, who is our home;*
> *Heaven lies about us in our infancy.*

A friend of mine was married to a colonel in the Seaforth Highlanders – one of the kilted regiments – a no-nonsense, down-to-earth sort of chap, I thought, until one day he said to me – and the sky wasn't especially strange and the day looked normal – 'I was a centurion at the time of Calvary.'

I looked round the room to see if anyone else was there and had heard. My friend, his wife, was sitting relaxed in a chair looking out through a french window. Her back view told me nothing.

'Oh really,' I said, the expression used when I was being diplomatic in Washington, the colonel's lady at a meeting near the barrack square, and quite often when I wasn't listening.

'I'll tell you about it,' he said.

This time I listened.

He revealed that he was a Buddhist in terms of belief. He reasoned (rather than believed) that the only thing that made sense out of man's presence on the planet was the *fact* of their continual return to it. 'Until they get it right,' he said.

I *was* listening to him, Peggy; but suddenly there flashed across my mind the picture of Jack Benny playing the violin on stage and receiving the applause with relief that it was all over, when a man at the back of the concert hall clapped on and on, the performer exhausting himself with encore after encore and saying finally to the hall: 'That's enough.'

From the back of the room came: 'You'll play on until you get it right.'

But to return to Buddhism, or at least to the

Colonel's interpretation of it, I wanted to ask him if he was a Buddhist at the time of Calvary. And what, after all, is 'getting it right'?

According to him it is the working towards the moment of jumping off the wheel of life. I feel 50/50 about this idea. It would be nice to merge with the Whole, particularly for artists who have been slaving themselves trying to show Him that He's not the only one to create, but with the other 50 per cent I can't help wondering why we ever broke away in the first place, or, to put it more honestly, why did He let us go?

The colonel told me more and more about his other incarnations – a sort of Walter Mitty life he'd been living. One of them was commanding troops. Then he said 'You realize, do you, that you are marked with the Cross. You are an Old Soul.'

Well! Before I understood that this is the language used between Buddhist followers, I was taken aback to think that my air of blonde well-being was hiding this ancient interior. He went on to explain that I was quite high up – or did he mean high round? – in the hierarchy of Old Souls. Apparently I've been on this Earth a time or two, and, he told me, so has Nick.

'What's the matter with Simon?' I said furiously.

'Nothing. He's not an Old Soul.'

I've spoken to perhaps a more scholarly Buddhist since those days, who told me there isn't reincarnation as interpreted by the colonel. It's something else – and from what I could gather – it's a huge intellectual leap. Buddhism is not so much a religion as a philosophy – which at a certain point may be the same thing. 'There are four basic truths,' he said, and I sat waiting hopefully to have the Meaning Of It All reduced to a sentence. He told me further that I must get *The Four Basic Truths*, written by a Buddhist monk in English.

I found the book in a shop in the Charing Cross Road – of course – and knew immediately that it was not going to be bedtime reading. The four basic truths are of such complication that if you have understood them at all you are half-way there. It's all mind, and that's probably how Man will end up, or down. As mind. After all, Christians are told in the Gospel of St John (the beloved) that in the beginning was The Word.

It's as well, Peggy, that I'm not actually *speaking* my thoughts; the room is crowded enough with all the flowers from those who love and admire you, you needing so much air to keep going at all. Your breathing these days is getting shorter. The intake, I mean. But you continue to sit, rather than to lie, in the sort of position that would go down well with the teachers of Hatha Yoga. I don't quite know how you manage it, but your body is a oneness of suppleness, the bones seem to be melting away.

I think I'd like to find out what made the Buddha – this hedonistic prince – feel he had something to pass on to the world that was actually going to help mankind, when, as we know now, the conception is way above the heads of most.

Ah! It's the monks who must be the communicators. They must bring the Buddha's teaching to a point of enlightenment for the ordinary person. It's interesting that Christianity works in the opposite direction: free will, the importance of the individual, the ego is encouraged. Buddhism teaches that the self has to go before we can *be*. It's hard on writers, painters, musicians who create from inside the ego. I must discover how creative a Buddhist is who has fully understood the four basic truths.

Peggy, if you yawn again I'll take it to be a better way of getting air. I can't accept boredom, so I'll just say that those selfish old Greek gods punished Prometheus, who, with his fire, may have ignited all art. I can *just* accept Pythagoras, because he found a basic relation between musical harmony and mathematics, and, as music is the most divine of the muses, I'll have to accept mathematics. Which, no doubt, you would say is big of me. However, if you put four peaches on the window sill to ripen and take away one, you'd be left with three – obviously – but what did you do with the fourth?

You were good at mathematics, rhythm, dancing, painting, talking, letting out explosions of both anger and laughter – and seeing behind the façades that people put up. You didn't pull the façades down – you saw that life was too dangerous for that – you put windows in the wall. I'm going to miss you one hell of a lot because I haven't known anyone quite like you, and . . . you were – are – a balance to me.

I want to start thinking what it is you'll be leaving

behind for us. And at the same time I'll try to think why your first return to Ulster was something of a disappointment. I drove you to two of your old homes. I took you to Kilkeel harbour, to see the boats coming in from a night of herring fishing, to the Black Rock at Ballymartin, and when we were back in Killowen you told me that none of it meant anything any more except as a lovely place to visit. I felt a sense of ... no, I felt remorse. I'd pushed a decision at you. I persuaded you to return to your Ulster childhood. I thought that the upsetting of your life by that little mistake in the tropics could be put right if you were given a welcome from the hypocrites who had stopped your return before. But I got it wrong that time: it was memory that you thought you wanted. In subsequent visits you've managed a merger of past and present, and have inhaled a touch of new-found happiness.

What you will be leaving behind is your accumulation of helpful attitudes from studying the human psyche, and helping people in a direction when there was none before. And the fun of your acquisitiveness: shopping with you is a pleasure.

'Go on. Get it,' you say. 'You know it suits you.'

'Well, I don't know.'

'Yes you do. It's the right colour for your eyes.'

'The same as yours.'

'Cousin dear, you are size 14 and I am size 8.'

And:

'Shall we have red wine, or white?'

'Both.'

You are leaving behind the golden young man who is your son. One eye is very slightly off centre which gives him a touch of mysticism, and as a financial director in a finance house it's just as well. You're not sure about John's wife Alicia – a fireball like yourself. But there are no doubts about their twelve-year-old, Julia, who has all the sexual seductiveness that as girls we were never allowed to show. I would like to think you'll see her grow up – to watch the battles between her and her mother. Julia is already beautiful, and John and Alicia will have a struggle with her, because, quite instinctively, she woos everyone.

So, in the meantime, we'll take a little journey west out of Kilkeel, travelling beside the square fields, passing the whitewashed cottages, away from the threat of bombs, shooting and alien Irishmen, and listen to the silence that is still a part of the Silent Valley.

But I have to tell you before we go bumping about in our little hired green car that I'm not all that fond of *too* much silence. It hits me worst when I wake in the middle of the night, say 2 or 3 o'clock, when there is the stark fear that the world may have stopped and you didn't manage to get off it with the rest of humanity. Death happens often around two in the morning. The body temperature is at its lowest. I wouldn't be surprised, Peggy, that *you* will decide the time of your departure.

Through the ages, Death has been painted as something evil, stealing up in the night – or day – by the rule of the Absolute Will, which is unyielding. But Christianity, of the humane kind, depicts it as the figure of Christ with his lamp leading you through.

You've asked not to be sent to your solitary room in Richmond when the time comes, with only Peter to care for you. You know, we know, that he couldn't manage it.

Some of the *caring* that we've acquired through the age of computers can be switched on with a button or knob. Peter does love you, Peggy, but can't show it. If there had ever been a chance of his exposing his feelings, public school and the Navy during the war took care of what might have been a little slip in the Establishment make-up. Don't think I'm knocking the Establishment; it was suitable when we were colonizing, sending our sons – usually the second – to outlandish places to look after the natives, giving them Christianity and keeping them in check. Who would want emotion in that sort of situation, as you swatted mosquitoes and drank your sundowner earlier and earlier each day? You had conversation with the other district officer whom you saw twice a year maybe; you gave orders to 'the boys' who looked after you, and you bedded down with whoever's daughter the natives decided would fit – if you see what I mean – but you didn't think about love.

As we know the areas of pink on the map of the world are vanishing, and with it the need for the essentially stiff upper lip (firm will now do), and before you know it the man who said to me: 'I suppose it's sex to begin with, then it's conversation' will be gone too. He was describing how he saw marriage, and, in a sort of way, was making a proposal. Yes, he had been to Eton, Cambridge and into the Grenadier Guards, but in his case it was long before then that his feelings were strangled. It began when he was a boy, had a wet dream one night at home, and was severely punished for it.

But we were talking about silence, Peggy, and I believe you now like it. I leave the door of your room open so you can hear movement up and down the corridor, and the odd word thrown cheerfully into the room. But when you know it is your cousin Pauline sitting here, you say: 'Shut it.'

So I'll talk about the flowers in your room, the ones perhaps you cannot see, and how some of their nodding heads are towards you, spreading pollen into the air, a faint scent, and all the warmth of the sender. It's the little one in the corner, an old-fashioned pink posy, brought by granddaughter Julia, that connects most. She picked them herself, came into the room and laid them on your chest. Then she pulled your night-dress apart and looked to see where the 'hurt' was, and said: 'Are they making it better?'

It's the bright colours you love; you've always liked life in the extreme. Whereas I go for Gwen John, it is Hockney for you.

I wonder if I were to bring a paint box now, brushes and a canvas, what you'd choose to paint. I think it would be the nurses. Nuala with her reds and purple, the nurses with black hands and faces and crisp white uniforms. Flowers you would not paint: they're better in the garden, you'd say. It's all part of the anti-slop. Old ladies sitting in delicate clothes and picture hats in a garden definitely is 'slop'. What isn't slop, Peggy? I'll tell you what is not slop: bringing up a son without a father because the father settled for permanent absence isn't slop. Seven years of training to be a doctor isn't slop. Losing the one person who was your equal – your brother Warren – probably at a time when you most needed him – is not slop. Squaring up to the first time you were told you had cancer and trying to put the specialist at ease wasn't slop. And, in latter years, insisting that other cancer specialists didn't use euphemisms when telling you about your condition is a very long way from slop.

You've become the favourite in this nursing home south of the Thames – because that's where you are, Peggy. You are not in some South American dump thousands of miles away.

Did you see Elizabeth Taylor and Richard Burton on stage together, playing opposite each other in *Who's Afraid of Virginia Woolf?* She stole the show early in the play when she walked onto the stage – a setting of a run-down sitting-room – saying to her stage husband, who was also her real-life one: 'What are we doing in this dumppp?' And the *p*, like a pistol shot travelling all around the theatre, reached Burton. He, great actor that he was, confirmed later that it was *her* play.

So that may have been in your mind when you arrived here, because yours, dear, dear Peggy, was an entrance, as if the Queen of the May herself had arrived, with at least three of her servants in trail.

You commanded us in childhood; you have commanded your husband, Commander Peter Holiday, RN; you organized – solely – John's growing-up; and all the time in a safe compartment of your being was this 'elf', as your friend, Jan, called it, picking up the messages from the 'otherness of man'. Don't tell me that the paradoxes in people aren't the most interesting aspect of personality.

Funny, isn't it, that only yesterday people reached for their guns when confronted by a psychiatrist. Mind you, at the root of their prejudice was a desperate need to be helped themselves. The judge who came to lunch at Killowen took a couple of steps backwards when he learned that you, Dr Peggy Fry, were an analyst, and I, Pauline Neville, was a writer. The poor man's poor wife had cancer also, about at the same stage as your own. And he could have trouble ahead for himself if ever those he'd sent into the Maze or Long Kesh came out.

When they arrived that afternoon it was an arrival of two cars. Judge, driver and security man in one; wife of judge, driver and another security man in the other. Make no mistake, the IRA have cost the authorities a lot of money.

The day was calm and beautiful, and the judge felt lulled, so when he decided he wanted a group photograph of us all in the garden, he called out: 'Paddy, come out of the bushes and take this snap.' Paddy was a charming security man, and didn't laugh to himself at the lapse as he came out of the bushes, because he knew that the judge's wits were as alert as his own.

It was when the judge wanted to go out of the garden and onto the shore that the detectives decided to split up. The barbed wire was removed, the clanging gates were opened onto the shore, and out we stepped, a line of Loyalist Protestants, a standing target for anyone who happened to be drifting past in the water.

'Can you believe it?' said you, under your breath.

And I whispered back: 'Luckily not fully.'

'But . . . !' Then you noticed two men dressed like Paddy – grey flannel trousers and blazers, revolvers strapped under the blazer – standing further along the shore, watching our every move. One of them lifted his arm, and our freedom was over. We were back behind the barbed wire, and it was into the cars for the judge and his wife, to the journey round Newry, to Belfast, and to the guards all round their house.

You were also there, Peggy, the night the Lord Chief Justice and his wife came to dinner. We were not told who was coming until ten minutes before their arrival.

Discussion in the sitting-room was between Gerald and Margaret: 'Should we leave the curtains open so that the judge and his wife can see the garden?'

'If the curtains are open and he sits in the window seat, he'll be a target.'

The view they were going to see is of a little path that winds between lawns to the gap in the hedge. Beyond the hedge, on a distant shore, is Eire, and at regular intervals the Marines' gun-boat on patrol.

'I don't think the poor man will have come all the way here to see British soldiers on a boat,' say you.

But you were not taking into account the blossoming of Margaret's garden in early summer, nor the smells that were coming in through the window, nor the fact that the journey from Belfast to Killowen was through territory a great deal more alien. It was one of your first trips to Ulster since childhood, and you hadn't yet steamed up the anger that was to come later on the subject of the IRA.

At dinner we discussed gardens generally, the Royal Family, the food, wine, Margaret's excellent shining table, with the cut glass looking even more cut than usual, and the silver reflecting faces as if there weren't already a number of looking-glasses in this lovely room. Sarah in her black dress and lace apron waited at table, Gerald following with the wine, and after we had the main course, and all were beginning to relax in the gentle evening breezes, Sarah came into the room, her hair dripping wet.

'Whatever have you been doing?' Margaret whispered.

'Ah, the tide was in, and I thought a quick bathe would cool me down.'

'But the barbed wire, Sarah?'

'Sure, Toby and I dealt with that.'

The Lord Chief Justice pretended he had not noticed Sarah's hair, because he knew sixty-nine-year-old Sarah had been with the family since she was fifteen, and nothing was going to unseat her. Besides, he had been told earlier that Loyalist Sarah had guns stashed away in the Mourne Mountains and under her bed, and would fight to the death to save everyone in the house.

I don't suppose I'll ever be able to decide where bravery ends and foolhardiness begins. Though I believe that for those who are sitting it out in Ulster, they have become more or less the same thing.

What bothers me now is the thought that you'll never be returning to this beautiful, always potentially dangerous place. But as we've unfrozen memory we can flit about in it, selecting, and editing if we wish.

I've noticed when talking to Americans that the expression 'going out there', meaning to the United States, is a bad reminder of colonial days when the British ventured into barbaric lands. So it's interesting to hear the Ulster folk refer to England as 'over there', as if they sensed *their* superiority.

I met the expression one evening when dining with nice, funny but reserved cousin Netta, who always managed to stir the pot and then sit back to listen. She lived alone since Dickie Mayston, a fellow student of Trinity and later her husband, died during an operation in London: the surgeons 'over there' for sure not knowing what they were doing.

Half-way through the dinner a guest opposite me at the table leaned forward: 'What do they think of us over there?'

'Do you really want to know?' I asked.

'Yes.'

'They think: a plague on both your houses.'

That did it. An explosion from across the table, and words tumbling out about: 'Who helped you in the last war? How many Ulstermen were killed?'

'I believe you were conscripted, like all the other available men in Britain.' You'd be surprised, Peggy, if you knew how like my English grandmother at times I can be, and no doubt will become. And don't forget when husband Michael was promoted from colonel to brigadier, and general later, I learned a thing or two about putting people in their place.

As it happens, I didn't want to put the dinner guest in his place, but I felt momentarily annoyed at the lack of logic in his thinking. Logic! did I say? But the result of my challenge was head-back laughter, and from him: 'Good girl, you've never lost the fight in you.'

That year when I was in Ulster on my own, and staying with Gerald and Margaret as usual, I felt the Troubles were troublesome. If nothing else can emphasize the English use of euphemism it's the expression 'Troubles' for the carnage that takes place.

In my borrowed car I was making my way through the mountains on one of the good roads, hoping to find a spot where I could park and walk. I came over the brow of a hill and almost immediately was onto a barricade. Surprisingly the brakes of the car were good, and I only just touched the bricks, stones, branches balancing there. I knew at once that it had been timed to get some particular person, or even convoy, reversed at full speed, swerved, and shot on down the road. At the nearest house that had a telephone wire, I stopped, rang the police, and sat down shaking.

I don't know if 'they' got their target because I went home by a different route, and nothing was given out on the news that night. I will not accept that they were waiting to get me. But I remember thinking, that year, about the conspicuous size and colour of me. The atmosphere, generally, was tense, and at meals, when lunching in other people's houses, we spoke guardedly, just in case there were Catholic maids in the kitchen who would be listening.

Of politics the dictionary says: '*Affairs of State*'. It also says: '*strife of rival parties*'. Ah, that's more like it. It does not say anything about prejudice and bigotry, nor does it mention the Church's role in it all. But today the Protestant Primate of All Ireland, the Archbishop of Armagh, in his fine cathedral, and the Roman Catholic Cardinal in his fine cathedral, are in accord in their understanding of 'strife of rival parties'.

Did I tell you, Peggy, what I read of Thackeray on the subject? 'I feel a sort of terror in going into a Catholic church, candles, altars and mysteries, the priest in his robes, the nasal chantings and wonderful genuflections will frighten me as long as I live.' Quite so. But we are, of course, talking about the DNA of prejudice.

I'll tell you what got me over all the fear connected with High Church. It was being sent to boarding-school in England, attending chapel twice a day, and on Sundays listening to High Church clergymen intoning in unnatural voices, and myself understanding that the reality was in the rows of giggling, whispering, sweating girls.

To the Ulster Protestants, Protestantism is a part of Britishness. But the absolute loyalty is to Ulster. Netta's dinner guest wanted to have it out with me about Whitehall.

'Whitehall comes between us,' he ventured.

I waited, having had a spell in Whitehall myself, and a clear memory of all the memos.

'It's Whitehall that has deserted Britain's friends all over the world. If Britain tries it on in Ulster – selling it to Rome via Dublin – watch out.'

Ulster, he continued, does not want talks with Whitehall about venues for further talks, it just wants to run the show herself – probably efficiently.

'And that includes dealing with the IRA alone,' I ventured.

'If the Brits weren't here, the IRA would stop.'

'You're a Brit yourself.'

He wasn't looking for answers. He just wanted to preach.

That year the police lookout posts in every town were like fortresses from the dark ages with only slits for windows and every movement of the citizens observed.

We have to understand that the people of Northern Ireland were being protected from each other – no one was ever quite sure. But, yes, you're right, it's the civil service that keeps continuity going. *Yes, Minister* sorted that one out for all time. The holy of holies has been revealed, the absolute centre of fix-it is known to all.

And sometimes I wonder, Peggy, how much of paperwork, in all departments, is necessary, and I think of the starkness of Father's desk when he had become chairman of the County Council. Committee meetings are for those who actually like paperwork, and lists, and 'Yes, Mr Chairman', and 'No, Chairperson', and I'll stop whispering to the colleague next to me when you stop repeating what we've just discussed.

The County Offices were in a listed building in the lovely town of Kirkcudbright. Artists came from all over the world to paint the town and the Solway Firth. We were lucky in childhood to be, as it were, a part of the beauty of place names, as well as places – sounds coming early into our heads, perhaps first through the river birds bringing in the morning. They say it's the light that brings the artists. It has a sharp softness, if the two can be combined – and they can – and light seems to play with the shadows as it does on the Mourne Mountains in County Down. Rockcliffe, where we mostly swam and picnicked, has a golden beach and the additional wonder of cliffs and rocks:

ancient rocks that are several cousins later to the magnificent Giant's Causeway in Northern Ireland.

It's interesting, isn't it, that giants still have a causeway. Who'd dare change the name? And did they come across to Scotland with their big strides, dropping rocks here and there?

Just occasionally, we could persuade Father to come to the sea with us and to picnic on the sand. He was restless on the shore, not liking sand in his sandwiches, and finding the beach tame as a vantage point for a bathe, and dreaming probably of the Black Rock and his stylish diving, even into old age. But he'd go in the water at Rockcliffe if only to get rid of the Scottish midges. You don't win against Scottish midges. It's quantity, not quality, and because Mother had extremely fair skin, they mostly went for her, and the poor lady went for the cigarettes as the only means of stopping them. Hating the cigarettes even more, she'd blow polite little puffs up into the air and to the flying grey mass around her.

I don't think Father was particularly good at delegating, and we are not certain how reticent he was in discussion.

'You know damned well he wasn't.'

'Ah. I remember you once told him so, and got the two sharp sides of his tongue.'

If you've been trained as a preacher you expect silence when you speak. If you've been born in Ireland you've got the gift of flattery to suit your own purpose. If you've also – perhaps like one of his heroes, Winston Churchill – been a reader, you'll be better with the words and references than most. He was liberal about our reading. We travelled from Galileo to Darwin, from Isaac Newton back to Job who dared to question God, and on to John Buchan, great story-teller that he was, and who wrote about Galloway.

His office was very stark. Where were the files? Where were the notepads, pens, pencils and pending trays? Where were the typewriters? I'll tell you why they weren't there – because all record was in Father's head. Just what it was like to work with a man like Father is another matter. My guess is – exasperating. He did not need to be briefed. So you might wonder why he went to an office.

I'll tell you why.

He hated the telephone, and wouldn't use it at home. He didn't like his own voice on it, because the remnants of his Irish burr might give the impression he was joking. He couldn't get quick facial expressions from the telephone, nor could he tell from it if people were telling the truth. When he became Chairman of the Health Committee for Scotland, he would catch the night train to London from Dumfries and beard Whitehall. In particular, of course, he would deal with the Minister for Health, and when I say deal, I mean just that. He'd catch the night train back to Dumfries, and twenty-four hours later, would be in his pulpit in his parish church wearing all his robes which hid the battle dress underneath, which in its turn was preparation for a military exercise he'd planned for later.

Just how he managed to lord it over all the veterans of the Crimean, Boer and Great War – as Battalion Commander – is probably explained as a combination of unfailing memory and unquestioned air of authority.

When I brought husband Michael for the first time to the Manse, he was startled that this cleric with a scholarly head was firing questions at him that might have come from the Ministry of Defence – then called War Office. Each night, after dinner, Father would insist that Michael take him all the way through the North African campaign, and any other sphere Michael had been in. Mother and I would sit in the music-room. If you think that was 'slop', Peggy, let me tell you that listening to Mother play her cello was a long way from slop, because the discords could be as powerful as the wonderful sounds she could occasionally get out of this ungainly instrument.

Today I have a tape of Pablo Casals playing a Catalan love song on the cello, and I have Jacqueline du Pré playing Elgar's Cello Concerto, and, yes, there's a lot of slop when I listen to these, but I prefer to call it a feeling of wonder that these two musicians has each understood something of the mind of the composer. I still feel that the sounds from the cello are akin to the crying of a soul in torment. Mother's playing was just that, and perhaps that is why I don't like to remember her playing. Sadness was a part of her make-up, but she might have been artistically lost without it.

I dwell on the subject of memory because mine is not for facts. As a good filing cabinet of events, my brain does not qualify. Images, smells, sounds, conversation, ideas have a priority position.

'What year were you in Kenya?' people ask.

'It was during the Mau Mau period.'

'Yes, I know, but what was the date?'

I bring a picture out of my mind – Simon's birth – add on six years, take that figure away from his present age, and I've got it.

Why did my father not instil into me the secret of memory? I'll tell you why: because he made a singular pounding of me every evening of the school holidays with spelling questionnaires. He never understood – people then didn't – that his daughter had a word problem. Agonizing tests in his study left me miserable and him frustrated, he believing that if only I'd concentrate a little harder I'd get it. He'd say: 'Write it down, and see how it looks.' Everything I wrote down looked all right to me. For Father, whose greatest love was for the English language, I must have been in those early years a big disappointment. As you'll remember, Peggy, he lived long enough for my English essay in what was called *Leaving Certificate, Oxford and Cambridge Joint Board*, to be given an A. But he was not, was *not* alive to know about the advent of my first book, *My Father's House*. Well, of course, he knew about my father's house, but he might like to have read how I experienced it.

All of this, Peggy, is to do with the memory bank

which you set up. You knew that facts would be no good, except for the fact of our club – exclusive to the four of us. You set it up with pictures in mind, so that feelings could also be remembered. It was to be the source from which we could draw. When the war came, shattering into our lives – and the knowledge of Warren's death – the bank, you felt, had to be set on ice, carefully guarded. But, unlike the stones on which we had written, it was not to be for posterity; it was to be for the conscious part of remembering.

Had you with insight sensed the nadir that lay ahead?

You've opened your eyes, the pupils large and opaque, and you are looking in my direction, but not *at* me.

'Has Robert been to see me?' you ask. The exotic plant by your bed has scented the room and the vision of a tropical night has followed. It is difficult to answer. The pain that that man has caused you has been nearly a negation of memory.

When Nuala has asked me about the night-time questioning I've told her about Robert, and she has reminded me that some happenings of an ambivalent nature *have* to be remembered.

Or 'Girl, dear, it's *her* memory now, not *yours*!'
Oh!

The smile that is flitting across your face is of something private between you and him. About time too, I suppose.

I'll have an independent thought about your mother: monsters can be liked when laughter turns into a giggle. How about the time she was told that some of the cattle around Ballymartin had been smuggled from across the border, twenty miles away. She, looking out of the window, said: 'I thought some of them looked very tired.' We, with the fixed image, thought of Aunt Netta's tired cows every time we saw them in any field the world over.

It was significant that she died in Ballymartin. A sort of homecoming, free of the bridge-playing friends in Belfast. It was cancer for her too, Peggy, all down one side of her. I wonder if the shock of Warren's death, just after peace had been declared, set her off. She was an ace at bridge but left it all behind to return to the setting for the great family gatherings.

I've been hard on your mother, Peggy, but now I can see that a girl with Victorian-minded parents, and seven brothers, all older, had to toughen herself to survive.

Mind you, it's not that I'm against bridge, it's something nimble for the mind, but I like to think that when the mind has been nimbled it does something with it. Bridge was a godsend when I was trying to dry out Richard (second husband – in case you have forgotten because he was with us such a short time). The nature of Richard was that he did everything absolutely. He was in the top league with maths and bridge, and he was in the death league with drink.

At about six months from what might have been the end, you suggested Alcoholics Anonymous: 'Patients of mine have been saved by them.'

'Well – I don't know.'

'There's got to be the will to stop.'

'I'm not sure he's got it. He doesn't believe he can manage without drink.'

'He'll be able to share his experiences.'

'It's too late,' Richard argued, downing his glass of gin in a gulp and giving me the usual sheepish smile.

'Give it a chance,' I said. 'It's killing you.'

You'd warned me not to push it too hard: 'Let it appear to be his idea,' you said.

He booked himself in with a specialist, and took me for the appointment. The specialist recommended a bed in his nursing home near Pinner, but warned us that there would not be a free one for about ten days.

'Ten days!' I cried, looking at the slumped body of Richard, all his defences down.

'This is what you'll do,' said the kindly man, who'd perhaps seen most of life's sorrows. 'Take him home and treat him as a patient – which he is. Bring him breakfast in bed with the cornflakes and the tea and the glass of gin.' There was no humour in his face. This was serious.

You telephoned: 'Make sure they don't use the aversion treatment.'

They didn't, and Richard went into the home, blind drunk on the day, but gentle and dignified as ever, and on Christmas Day being allowed out to a Christmas lunch of no Christmas pudding, no mince pies, but Simon and Nick having prepared a stocking for him. Richard arrived in a taxi, and coming into the kitchen, asked me not to hide my glass of whisky from him. I pulled it from behind the tin of biscuits – yes, it was the old one from *Inglis* – and let him pour me another, and learning that the dry alcoholic must be allowed to pour drinks and talk about drink as much as he likes.

The strain of sobriety got to him in the end, and winning at bridge only boosted him for a time. He began an affair with the bar girl in a wine bar who was *not* watching for the signs: the smell on the breath, and, in time, from the pores of his skin. The poor man sank into a desperate state, as before, and in the end his tired heart giving out under the strain of so many drink-related illnesses. The girlfriend and her husband came to the funeral, making a fuss of Simon and Nick – and they learning a thing or two outside boarding-school. I tripped over my feet going down the aisle as I heard the coffin slide away, and said to the black smoke that curled up from the crematorium: 'I understand, Richard, I really do.'

Gentle, kind people do get battered, Peggy, and I don't blame any of them for finding life too much, and the bottles of booze on the increase, day following day. Simon and Nick and I had dry tears together. Some feelings are too deep for the wet ones. But we all knew we loved Richard.

'I always thought the Colonel was too grown-up

for you,' say you, sliding slowly into one of your yoga positions, your eyes tightly shut. 'His conversations with me were out of Army Manual 264 on how to talk to wife's cousins.'

'It was the limp, Peggy. He came limping into the bookshop where I was starting my career "in books".' Richard waited a further fourteen years for my telephone call that came in the end; I knew that his voice was soaked in gin. His great friend said: 'You could save him from all of this,' and I, everybody's fool, believed it, and took him on, and realized that I was in on a decline, praying to the God who I'd often abused to give strength to us both.

It's not God you want today, Peggy, it's your Mother, that woman who was a monster to her children, but who taught you all to stand on your own feet. I'll tell you what Brendan Behan had to say about parents and children: 'Ach, once you've left home, you're out of it. Listen, you might as well expect the Ford car coming off the ramp down on the factory floor in Cork to turn round and say thank you.'

So when parents go on wondering and worrying and interfering with their grown-up children, it's self-indulgence. Your *Mammy* may have got it right when she left you all to get on with it. But she had not, had *not* got it right when she denied the existence of your son; it was a sanction of hypocrisy: accepting the standards of her bridge-playing friends and denying the truth. And, while we're at it, what about those strange, tall, dark good looks of your younger brother Paul? Did Aunt Netta ever explain that?

But your son today is giving you all the love you could want. He's on the telephone to me every day to see what we can do to make you a little less uncomfortable. He sits in his office working out complicated sums, but is thinking about you. And when I say 'thinking' his is actively sharing in your dying.

For now we can go back to root out the little moments that we can still share but have forgotten, and the one that reappears is the visit each year to the TT car race in Ulster. We rose early, travelled quickly and dangerously – if Uncle Humphrey had anything to do with it – to Newtownards, to the best position we could manage at one of the corners, in order to watch the real skill of driving. The personalities of the drivers communicated themselves to us so that when I was only four I asked if the English team leader could come back to tea at Ballymartin. When Mother said no, I asked her why not – it seeming then, as now, that he might have liked tea down by the Mourne Mountains, with Mary baking pancakes, sugar and butter on top – and for goodness sake, why not?

'A matter of fifty miles,' as Mike only recently pointed out.

We had our own in-law racing-driver from Canada. It was the first streamlined car we had been close to, and we raced up and down the long straight road near Ballymartin, hens, dogs, cats jumping out of the way, and your scarf, Peggy, getting caught in the works. The smell from the exhaust, the wind through our hair, the driving goggles steaming up, all adding up to an excitement that can be sensed today.

It was obvious that as the children of Humphrey Fry, you, Warren and Paul would have the racing bug in you; Mike and I echoed you.

Cars for Father were objects that took you to places, and they were nothing else. At the end of every month our Vauxhall was taken to the garage in Castle Douglas, and Father saying to the man: 'Do what you have to', and the foreman for certain finding something to do.

While waiting for the car to be repaired he went to the County Library to see Mrs Brown. Mrs Brown was a lady large in width and small in height. There were sweat creases down the side of her nose, and she gave the impression that she'd just walked to the top of a hill, which she had. Occasionally Father would drive her around the county distributing books to the various smaller libraries. After his wife, his children and his dog, Father liked Mrs Brown; she was the keeper of the only possession Father sought. He'd return from the library carrying a small leather brief-case, empty of all County Council papers but full of books. He would put the case on the small table in the study. It spoiled it for him if we got into the case first. So we made sure that the little brown case was not opened, and there was no resentment because we knew that in time the contents of the books in one form or another would be shared with us.

❖

When you lie with your eyes open, Peggy, I wonder what you're thinking. Are you, perhaps, sorting out the sequence of your life? Do you want to be brought back into the present moment?

What, for instance, did you think of our sons? I always wanted boys – girls had been the sort of strangers I met at boarding-school, whereas the first boy I knew and loved was my brother.

It's always been easy to find games that suit both brother and sister, if one is prepared to become a part of the other. I – more or less – assumed the persona of a boy. I won't go so far as to say I suffered from penis envy, though I think squirting urine in competition with Mike into the River Dee, knowing he would win, might be seen as such. Mike has told me, in recent years, that he had always seen me as a tomboy.

Your son John, as well as my two, Simon and Nick, can see a joke when it comes their way. I'd say that John's humour borders on satire, but then his life of question marks has left him that way. Simon has the kind of humour that can baffle strangers. He keeps a straight face when he's being clever with phrases, while Nick, much the same as your Uncle James, crumples with laughter, particularly if the joke has come from him. I think I've said it before, but I knew my two would have to find wives who'd stand up to them. And they have.

Isn't it strange, Peggy, when a wind that has been blowing for days stops? There is the territorial song of the birds, and then silence. Nature waits for the descent of night when all creatures – with a few wide-eyed exceptions – can be safe from the hunt. But, of course, it's absurd to say that the same thing happens night after night. Nothing is absolutely the same, from moment to moment. Today isn't like yesterday, and if today met itself the day after, it wouldn't recognize itself. All change, the bus driver would say, the next stop is morning – of the new day.

The four seasons – spring, summer, autumn, winter – are like the four divisions of day – morning, afternoon, evening, night. As we know, there isn't an afternoon in Ireland, and perhaps this is why so many of their calculations have gone wrong. The *whole* of Ireland, Peggy, is populated with *individuals* – some on the breadline – but chatting away to each other. In the South there's no fixation with time; there are days when it's practically destroyed. But not so in the North where 'good work' is one of the favourite expressions. It means 'well done' in a working sort of way.

When I speak to cousin Margaret on the telephone from London, almost everything I tell her gets 'good work', and she means it, especially if I've been sitting at the typewriter all morning and running committees in the afternoon. Margaret – ninety years old now – is still in her mind preparing briefs and generally looking after the clients she has had for about sixty years. Not that all are the original members of the family. She likes to think she is working for the grandchildren of her early clients, and as proud as punch to tell them so. The answer to almost everything in Margaret's terms is hard work. Law firms from Lincoln's Inn in London used to telephone her in her office in Newry about certain legal matters. It was said of her that she was still the best brain in her firm, full of young men.

If you wished to consult Margaret in her office in Newry, you'd have to walk up two flights of stairs, brass rods still on them, passing the door of ladies who had been there almost as long, and the greeting: 'Hullo Pauline' sending you on up to the third floor, with the welcome inside you. Margaret's room, which the office keeps open for her, is large and sparsely furnished. She sits, pencil poised. The layers of dust that greet you in solicitors' offices generally seem to have moved, in this case, up to the ceiling. The office itself has a scrubbed look, with hard-backed chairs, linoleum on the floor, and windows that have been stuck ever since the IRA took to bombing Newry.

The only days that Margaret has not appeared in her office are those when she didn't feel well and Sarah saying 'No' to Margaret walking towards the car. She continued working through security checks, road blocks, the sound of flying glass, and the sinister thud that excavates the ground, because her duty is to keep going and show the bastards – though she'd never use such a word – they're not going to win in Ulster. Besides, there are her clients, and if they can – and will – get in to Newry to see her, then she'll be there to greet them.

Her lunch goes in a box: two sandwiches, an apple and a thermos of coffee with boiled milk in it. She is not of the kind that takes clients out to lunch and waste the firm's money, she is the solicitor who uses her lunch hour to sit back and review the morning's work. If she had wanted to take the clients out to lunch she would have to travel a bit – out of the war zone, one might almost say.

Make no mistake, Peggy, Newry is a pretty awful place.

Our grandfather made his money there, don't forget.

So, you'd walk into Margaret's office, having given a discreet tap on the door, and sit opposite her on the other side of her large flat-topped desk, and she removes her heavy horn-rimmed spectacles, and you are dazzled by the blue-violet of her eyes. She knows about them, of course, and has chosen her clothes accordingly. Subdued mostly, but with a fleck of peacock blue here and there.

Anyone who made the mistake of thinking her feminine appearance and charming manner were all there is to it would be making a big mistake. She is sharp in the extreme; gets your point immediately and indicates she does not want you to labour it. You will be shown out of the office by her, whether your bill is going to be £40 or £400. She has time for everyone, and it may be because she is of value to Protestant and Catholic alike that her office is intact.

She does not actually have Catholics working in her office – that would be letting liberalism go too far – but she has got as many of them out of scrapes as she has the Protestants. On the other hand, cousin John Fisher – grandson of eccentric Uncle Frank – and his father Jim before him, employed both Protestant and Catholic in their ever-expanding business. The huge lorries used to travel around the country with J. S. FISHER in large white print on them, so it was obvious to the world – or the IRA if you like – that they were not hiding.

I was going to remind you, Peggy, about the time our cousin Netta was out of the house doing some good works with the Red Cross. She lived alone in Seven Steps after Dickie died, and employed a maid who was Catholic, perhaps as a guarantee. It paid off. On this particular day she was out, and the Catholic maid happened to be looking out of the window – a fond pastime in these mainly rural areas – when she saw a man with a familiar face walk coolly up the outside steps and place a package on the top one. He left in a hurry, and Bridie, her instinct telling her the worst, rushed out of the room, opened the front door, and, picking up the bag, went to the back of the house and threw it with all her strength to the bottom of the garden. It exploded at once. Although it was not a powerful bomb it managed a large hole in the ground, the destruction of the greenhouse and the devastation of the garden.

So, the world might ask, what had Netta done to warrant such singular attention? Her husband, a Protestant clergyman, had become a padre to several British regiments, finishing his career as Deputy Chaplain General in the British War Office. His photograph was all over the house, and the sword from the dress uniform was used in the sitting-room to poke the fire.

Her Catholic maid had saved her life, and she was probably the one who'd prevented the Provos when they came on an earlier day – men in white coats in a white van – from taking away even more of her good furniture.

Before you returned to Ulster, I stayed a few days in Seven Steps. Netta and I would go shopping together to pay the newspaper bill in one of the shops.

'Oh, hullo Mrs Mayston. How's yourself?'

'Just grand, Kevin, just grand. How's your wife and kids?'

'They're grand.'

'This is my cousin, Mrs Neville, staying with me.'

'Over from England, then?'

We walked out of the shop, and Netta said: 'He's active in the IRA.'

'I like your friends.'

'We've got to live beside them.'

So, it's respectable clothes by day and into stockings over the face at night.

One day a visitor from England, driving her own

car, stopped in the middle of one of the small towns to ask for a petrol pump. Some men closed in on her, their expressions threatening. 'If you don't go away, I'll send for the police.' Her accent was worse even than her English car number plate.

'For the polis! Here?'

Stories like this get around, and it increases the vigilance, but surprisingly not the fear. Anger is a better word.

That summer Netta lent me her car to get around. I returned it to its garage, just up the hill, on the day I was leaving. As I approached the garage I could see written in large white paint: BRITS KEEP OUT.

If you think you're anonymous over there you'd be wrong.

Two years ago, Peggy, we saw Netta for the last time. She insisted on having you to stay for a couple of days, and during that time she organized that a party of us would go out to dinner in the one restaurant left standing. No, she would not be coming with us, but she'd have everyone in for drinks first, and, no thank you, she would not have a drink. She just wanted to see us all, friends and relations. She was wearing an aubergine-coloured skirt and pretty shirt, the ruff high up her neck. She hardly talked, but she was the hostess. She saw us off, having arranged with the restaurant that the bill be sent to her, and her guests were to choose anything they liked that was on the menu.

The following day we were on our way to the airport, and Netta was calling for a taxi to take her to a nursing home just outside Newry. She died a few days later.

Guts, did you say?

It's there, written into everything they do, a high level of fortitude and single-mindedness. Netta wanted to thank you, Peggy, for looking after her in London when Dickie was in hospital, and the rest of us for being her friends — as well as her relations — and for the fun we'd had together. Her manner of going was what we would have expected: quick, neat, full of understanding of her own possibilities.

Good-bye, Netta. You were great.

It's going to be Margaret next, because she's been dropping hints. There will be no fuss, of course, and, if it were to happen while we're back in England, she'll have given no indication of its imminence because at the time of departing she'll have said: 'See you next year.'

That's the way to deal with the whole subject. All a part of *living*.

Nuala has been in again with her ribald ballad: '*But a sudden awe of the angry law/Struck his soul with an icy chill/So to finish the fun so well begun/He resolved himself to kill.*'

'Did I hear you talking to yourself?' said she.

'I was talking to Peggy.'

'Didn't I tell you that it's not words she's after now?'

'What then?'

'Loving.'

'She'd know something was up if I suddenly put my arms around her.'

'Girl, dear, it's now or never.'

That's Nuala. An amazing combination of irreverence and Christian loving. She'll be the one with you at the end. Or, as she'll see it, the beginning.

Just the other day I took James Joyce out of the library – *Ulysses* of course – the first time, when I was fighting dragons, it was too much for me. This time I could hear him, because it's prose music we're listening to. Did you know the man had a fine tenor voice? Listen to this, hearing perhaps his voice: 'A barmaid, for the amusement of a rake, let free in sudden rebound her nipped elastic garter smackwarm against her smackable woman's warm-hosed thigh.' Do you feel, sometimes, that the great writers are giving us a language in addition to the one we already have – rich, deep-rooted?

Ulysses is to be broadcast on Radio 4, in sixteen episodes, at 11.30 p.m. I'll get Nuala to turn on your radio and we can listen to it together.

Why don't we turn on your radio now? It would be a presence for you in between visits. Peter and John can only come in the evening.

It's confusing to have the two Johns in the family, but your John, Peggy, has only just become family-minded. He's avoided Ireland over the years because of your treatment there. He's lumped all the relations together – not fully understanding that it was only his grandmother who'd dismissed his existence. It's only now that you're going, possibly taking all

contact with Ulster with you, that he's turned to me.
I think I can introduce him to the real Ireland, and
the warmth that comes from the people who live
there. It took you a few years of coming back to
Ulster before you could even talk about your son.
Four years later you had to let slip that John has a
partner, and between them they have five-year-old
golden Julia.

Julia has asked: 'If Grannie dies, will the angels
take her to heaven?' – leaving John and Alicia with
a problem, because Alicia, a psychotherapist, is
against all religions, and John – well John just hopes
there is something for his mother to go to.

You've encouraged me, Peggy, to talk about
cancer, to say the word out loud. The reason why
you've been handling it as well as you have is
because you've drawn back the curtains on the
subject. And you've told me that it is all to do with a
rogue cell getting above itself and multiplying,
taking over – you might say gone on an ego trip –
sufficiently pleased with itself to want mirror images,
and none of it, *none*, in your favour. I know you talk
to the rogue cell, and for quite a time you were on
an equal footing, word for word, pain for pain. In
the last year and a half, exhaustion has weakened
you, and the multiplying has run amok. Scientists do
not yet know how the rogue cell reproduces itself.
Science knows about the double helix, and how the
genes are passed on, but it does not know just how
this rogue cell gets the strength to do what it does,
and with what.

For two years I was a Friend to the Westminster Hospital and worked in the surgical cancer ward. My brief was to go round the wards with a small watering-can, topping up plants, taking away dead flowers and giving fresh water to struggling ones. It was, of course, a way of starting conversation with the patients. If there's one thing I've always managed quite well, it's the starting of conversation. It's having a shy mother that did it. If the two of us were together and meeting others, I was the buffer: the little chattering daughter. So, in these wards I'd walk from bed to bed, bringing in the outside world to this enclosed area of doubt and fear. Any old bit of sunshine would do, and it gave the patients the chance to look you over, find out if they could trust you, and then alight on a topic. Quite often it was about their families encased in photograph frames near the beds; it was the grandchildren that got through to me because they'd come sometimes into the ward. Enlightened parents would realize that their children *should* (dare I?) know about most of the facts of life. The shock of what they might see could be got over in their lifetime. For a neglected grandparent there is no time.

There was one grannie, short grey hair, plump, a smile that reached from ear to ear, who said: 'Aren't I lucky, my daughter is coming to take me home.' I handed her the feeding cup that had just been passed to me, and saw that she had no arms. She was lying on top of the bed, with her one leg – the last of her limbs. It was a crisis for me, and I wanted to rush from the room and scream. The patient helped me through it. She said: 'Don't upset yourself, dear, it's been going on a long time. It'll be over for all of us soon, but I won't be alone when it happens.'

So I talked to her about my grandchildren – at the time one of six and one of four. Yes, I do carry photographs in my wallet, just in case. We compared hers and mine, and I think the fact of those children was the aspect of her life that she holds on to.

The patients on either side of her in the ward benefited from her attitude. I believe that they were fed by the absolute goodness that was in this woman. What I shall never know is whether goodness came upon her because of the fortitude that came with the illness, or whether she was one of those who come into this life blessed.

What was a great deal more painful was the seventeen-year-old girl who was also in a terminal condition and could neither accept nor forgive the world for her illness. She gave the staff, the other patients and her parents, a very rough time. The parents came twice a day bringing more, yet more, woolly animals, when all she wanted was a passport to get out of her condition. She could not accept that her life was going to stop when there was so little of it behind her. She screamed at everyone. But led by the grey-headed lady, the other patients in the ward refused when the offer was made to move the girl. In the end, in a way, they all saw her through.

There were some small rooms attached to the big ward that only special nurses and doctors could visit.

I still ask myself the question: if I had been told I could visit these patients, would I have done so?

Do you know, Peggy, that it is evening again, and the little birds are back. Scuffling about in the gravel, cleaning their wings.

I've always been fascinated by the apparent freedom of birds: they are alone of the many species that can take to the air. They can travel distances with an in-built radar system that man cannot comprehend. Cows, for instance, eat all under the condescending permission of man; sheep do the same; the wild animals are bound by their mistress: earth. Man can imitate the bird by the ever-enquiring nature of science — but study cows standing in the river on a hot summer day, the reflection touching the shore, the midges in dense clouds hovering, and you have the abstraction of art into a dimension that nothing or no one controls.

I didn't know when I was on my way to you this morning I'd hear seagulls. I listened to the screaming discord of their cry, and for an elongated second — that second that gives many a novelist inspiration — I was back in that little bedroom at Ballymartin with the sun filling the room, an open invitation to rush out of bed and join the fun. But I stayed where I was, well up the River Thames, and drank of memory.

The legend, as we know, is that the cry of the seagull is the cry of the sailor taken by the sea before his time, and, like the Flying Dutchman, is forever seeking – not for a port to land, but for the body of the sailor from which the soul has been separated.

As children we learned the cry of the different seagulls. And only as children could we imitate it. Is sound as evocative to the mind as is smell to the nose? Or is it itself remembered?

I don't believe children ever walk down a staircase; it's a bump, bump on the stairs, or a slide, slide down the banisters, or, even more dangerous, a jump from the top to the bottom. My particular jump led to the scar today on my forehead, and, at the time, the concern from Mike: 'No one will want to marry her now.' I think I was six at the time, Mike around nine and a half. As you get older, speed down staircases – or anywhere else for that matter – slackens, because you have realized that the years behind you are outnumbering the ones in front.

Your Uncle James, Peggy, had little knowledge of the ageing process, for himself. He stayed young, and ignored the aches and pains. In his life he spent only one day in hospital, having a cyst removed from the top of his ear, and in the evening was making a speech at the Home Guard dinner. My today picture of him is of a slightly stooped figure, exuding a quantum of energy of the cerebral nature, walking as if there was not much time before his death, aged eighty-three. Did he know? Certainly in the last year of his life he would have Mike in his dressing-room going through the papers in his desk.

I think my earliest memory of Mother and Father is in Ballymartin, the two of them changing in the shore behind large wrap-around towels, and stepping into bathing suits of outstanding ugliness.

'Did yous remember to put in the rubber shoes?' That would be Mary, handing over the towels and bathing suits from the pulley in the kitchen. To get to the Point Sands you had to walk over several hundred yards of stones of a variety fit for a museum. Mother had delicate feet, in the same way she had delicate almost everything else, and getting her across the stones – even wearing the rubber shoes – was done with a certain amount of serious-ness in case she wouldn't come at all. Having been pushed into the sea by Father at the Black Rock was a reminder to her that the Irish, when they want, can be a bit rough.

The crunchy dark-brown sugar of the sand out there was a parade ground for more than us bathers. Gulls would strut, water snipe and sandpipers, beaks busy in the sand, their jagged feet making patterns we tried to imitate.

The first bathe in every August was usually from the Point Sands, and you, Peggy, were the first to go, rushing across the stones as if they were wood chippings put there for you. Screams of delight and splashes, then the nearly equivalent rush from Mike, followed up by the slower plod of Warren and myself.

Lowering the body into the Irish Sea is like a descent into broken glass, but once you're in, up to the neck, the pull of the waves takes you back and forth, already a part of the motion.

Looking back at it now, I suppose it's not surprising that we played with stones, Peggy. The northeast part of Ireland is the part of the world that nature uses as a canvas. A drawing-board for the divine pencil. A magnet to archaeologists, and indeed architects, from all over the world. Painters too. It was sitting at the head of Giant's Causeway that the four of us, once war had been declared, made the promise to return to the exact spot, if we survived. We took photographs of each other. There may have been something prophetic that only three could be photographed at any one time.

When we were in our teens, the parents bought us bicycles. The roads seemed designed mostly for pedestrians, the chatter of them going up and down, 'Sure it's cold enough today to confuse even the fish in the sea', and we crashing round corners, our arms free, following the richness of our imagination, and coming in for the last lap of the TT motor race. We can be glad of the benefits of our Anglo-Irish background, but I believe that the inheritance is with the Picto-Celts who were responsible for the moulding of minds that plucked playing out of the air. Stones: stones lying there to be taken up and used for our purpose was an indication to the young mind that each stone could be anything we liked. I don't believe we were particularly competitive. It was all done in the cause of discovery, and pleasure.

You have told me from time to time that you were

bad when you were a young girl. What badness could there have been? Were you banking up revenge against your mother? Were you cheating on your brothers? I can't believe it was fumbling sex because the incident in the summer house must have dried up the juices for a decade or two. Or were you simply defying every instruction you were ever given? 'No. No. I won't.' In your teens you had a way of walking on your heels when you were at your most defiant, head slightly in the air. And 'I won't grow up just because you want me to.' But I'm happy to say, Peggy, that a part of you never has. Today we know about the grown-up side that is coping with your illness, the imagination staying young and free, Blake's 'Divine right of the imagination of which the Vegetable Kingdom is but a faint shadow', saying something of it.

When we weren't on our bicycles we were climbing the mountains, Slieve Binian the favourite. We'd been promised duck eggs for tea by a small farmer on the way up. I was still wearing my St Trinian's school sweater, hoping that the thing would be torn to shreds on the bilberry bushes, when Warren announced he wanted to bathe.

Little mountain streams trickled down on all sides of us, transparent water showing the plant and animal life within, and, our hands cupped, we drank and drank, until you said to me: 'Take that thing off.'

'No. I want it torn by the bushes.'

'Try the stream.'

So, off it came, and Warren, stripping, put a leg

into each sleeve and was in the water sliding up and down, the miserable garment left in shreds on the mountain, and I later having to save my pocket money to buy a new one.

Duck eggs turned out to be turkey eggs, and just try putting a turkey egg inside the traditional egg cup. The farmer's wife lifted down the old black frying pan, dolloped in beef dripping and broke in the eggs, one at a time, each filling the pan to look like a water lily in a dark pond. They were Protestant turkeys, of course.

We were scarcely out of our teens when rumours of the war came intruding into our sheltered lives. First to go was Mike, called up into the army; you next, with your doctorate, to the WAAFs; Warren to follow, his doctorate, and into the RAF; and Pauline back to school between Reading and London – and night after night of no sleep because of the Germans: drone, drone, drone above, and in time recognizing the different sounds of an aeroplane *with* bombs, and without. Actual killing had not come into our thinking, except – oh yes! – Mary dropping live lobsters into a pan of cold water – keeping their colour that way – and watching as the pan slowly came to the boil. The Nazi horrors had not infiltrated into the absorbing process of growing up.

Not so your Aunt Marj, Peggy, who, having lost a cousin and a gentleman friend in the Great War, was appalled to find that we would be fighting them again, and possibly this time on home ground. Years later when I bought my VW she was not pleased. It's interesting, isn't it, how the apparently meek can have great areas of anger when it comes from prejudice. When I drove her about in the VW she'd look straight ahead out of the window, pretending, I suppose, that she was safely back in Father's old Vauxhall.

Today you can sit in that special chair they have brought in for you, issuing orders, dreaming about childhood in Ballymartin, and wondering if all that holidaying through the world was a search for the lost innocence. Don't wonder, Peggy, it's still there, and the drug you have been put on to now makes you nod and smile as if all creation is yours, while I tell you about The Holy Church of the Apostles, near my flat here in London. Bells ring at 7 a.m. and at midday. The Catholic community attend Mass twice a day, and, I'll say this, come out smiling, talking to each other and throwing quips over their shoulders in the Irish tongue. Yes. One of the priests, who also rides a bicycle, spends a part of his day on it, his pipe clasped between his teeth, his smiling eyes everywhere, the red face telling the generosity of his parishioners.

I met him at dinner, Peggy, given by some English cousins.

'Hullo.'

'Hullo. Haven't I seen you somewhere before?' This not being the usual approach with a man of the cloth, I added, 'Perhaps in Ulster?'

'Do you know the Church of Holy Apostles?'

'Of course.'

'I have my home there.'

At dinner I was put next to him.

'D'you ever go to Ulster?' said I, because he had been introduced to me as Father Russell.

'I do.'

'So do I.'

'Which part?' said he.

'Do you know Rostrevor in County Down?'

A nod from him.

'Well, come out from Rostrevor on the coast road going north and in about a mile you come to . . .'

'Killowen? I'm one of the Russells of Killowen.'

'But . . . but I thought they were Protestants.' Did I hear the old prejudice in my voice?

'People can change.'

Thank you, I said to myself, for not adding 'to the *true* faith.'

During dinner I told him about my life in Galloway in Scotland, in a Scottish Manse, and coming to Ulster each August, and about my father's stipend when he began in church work of £400 a year, and how my English grandmother paid for our schooling.

'He was lucky,' said Father Russell, the grin growing.

'Would you have preferred less?'

'D'you know nothing at all?' said he, and I knew that he'd never really left Ireland.

'Sometimes I think not,' said I, determined to be part of the fun.

'We do not have stipends in the Catholic church.

Priests are servants of the people, and we are
dependent upon their bounty.'

'Good God!'

'Yes, indeed.'

'Is this to keep you humble?'

'It's to keep us the same.'

But they're not the same, as we know, Peggy. I'm
determined to hang onto my prejudice for a little
longer, though much more of Father Russell and I'll
be lighting candles.

I've tried to think if it's prejudice that I'm still
slightly afraid of. A play put on at the Royal Court
some years ago, *Hadrian VII*, brought one of my
fears out into the open. Coming from the back of
the theatre some time in the middle of Act 2 were
actors dressed in clerical robes, swinging containers
of incense. I was back into childhood, and the fear
even of the exterior of the Roman Catholic church,
and dreading the power that it might have over me.
There was no escape from the smell because the
performers walked slowly down to the stage, the
whole audience either squirming or in ecstasy. I'll
take my thinking further, Peggy, and suggest that
the fear of incense is to do with the fear of being
taken over; the ego about to be damaged, or worse,
absorbed. This then the policy of the Catholic
Church, the subjugation of the Self to the Will of
God, as I saw it.

Do you remember the old organ in the Mourne
church? I swear to God (you see!) the same woman
has been pumping the air into it through the Christian

ages; arms and legs flexed, small hat tilted to the side, her mouth opening and shutting, as if to give timing to the congregation but the sounds in competition with the actual music. This, it seems to me, is more to do with the religion of the people. Prejudice? Yes.

I think I place music appreciation the highest in the order of the senses. Aristotle – if you'll forgive the comparison – placed sight highest, because, as he said, the eye is closest to the brain from which comes the analytical faculty. Plato – while we're at it – put touch at the bottom because it's nearest to the instinct.

No? I knew you wouldn't agree. After all it's a touch relationship you have with all textiles, inventing them in your mind into clothes of rare excitement, and the knitting of huge coats and jackets, and the never wearing of them. Aunt Netta must have ultimately found her sensuous daughter quite hard to accept.

I stumbled on a manifestation of the power of touch once when following a group into the Tate Gallery; we were swept into a dark room, only the smallest of lights showing in one corner. Those in front of me were deciphering changes of surface with their fingertips, grateful for the heightening of sensitivity, and making cerebral assessments, as they *experienced* this Rodin exhibition of pieces of sculpture there in this room darkened especially for the blind.

So, Peggy, mistakes, like accidents, even at the hand of the Almighty, aren't always mistakes. They're propelled by an inner force that has little to do with external happenings. If some of this is heavy upon you, let me say that much of the analytical perceptions have come from you.

Let me tell you about some of my own stupidity mixed with arrogance. I *made* my parents cancel my music lessons at school because the Mozart Clarinet Quintet was not immediately tripping off the ends of my fingers. Later I *expected* to grasp Einstein's Theory of Relativity. I even wondered if I might find God at the centre of the split atom. I'll tell you something I have learnt while browsing round the world, in and out of bookshops and libraries: Jewish literature has nearly got the monopoly of God. Writers' Day at the Festival Hall one year had a writer from Israel as guest speaker. He had us listening to his confirmation that God is there at the dipping of the pen into the ink, at the crossing out of mistakes, at the birth of a better idea . . .

Has it ever occurred to you that humans would be *entitled* to a bit of paranoia?

I wonder if what you were doing in the early part of your life was seeking out the one quality of nature that is a fixture – the speed of light? Were you rushing through the universe in search of union? Or were you perhaps that one-off beam of light that came riding in on a rainbow?

'Oh good, Peggy, I have made you simulate laughter. But, please don't try to get out of that chair, your spirit *will* escape.'

'Who says?'

'Your common sense.'

'My . . . what?'

▓

Following your first cancer operation, we went for a week of luxury to Reid's Hotel in Madeira. We only slept there because the air inside the hotel was as expensive as the food. Can you believe that we had four bath towels each, fresh every morning, and the sheets changed twice a day. *What* were we supposed to be doing in them in the middle of the day? Mind you, judging by the average age of the guests they probably *slept* in the afternoon, waiting for the next meal.

You asked the hotel to call you one morning early in order the watch the *Queen Elizabeth II* sail into Funchal harbour – the second largest port in the world. You were putting into play the very infectious Irish 'Sense of Occasion'.

The telephone by my bed rang.

'Hullo?'

'Wake up, it's five in the morning and the boat will be in in half an hour.'

'It's still dark outside, Peggy.'

'The captain will handle that.'

'For God's sake, this is no time for jokes.'

'It's no joke getting a great ship into harbour.'

'I'm going back to sleep.'

'Well don't ask me to tell you anything about it.'

'I won't.'

We were sitting on a snack-bar stool in Funchal, sipping Madeira, the local wine, when you said: 'I know there's *something*.'

You'd just been examining the purple of the

jacaranda trees – trees of sweet-smelling wood – and at the same time dismissing a pain from the newly operated breast. You'd seen beauty and felt ugliness at the same moment. Your thinking on mortality was in and around what we saw and did on that holiday. The fact that you were able to shelve it for a number of years said a lot for your 'there's something', and the something probably sustained you when it all came back again.

'When you actually have cancer it removes the terror of getting it.'

'Oh! Peggy!'

Osip Mandelstam's widow's written word says something of it: 'When all hope has gone, there is nothing else to fear.'

Nuala is back with her ballad as she straightens your chair: '*Then he took the sheet/off his wife's cold feet/and he twisted it into a rope/and he hanged himself from the pantry shelf/'Twas an easy end, let's hope –/in the face of death/with his latest breath/he solemnly cursed the Pope.*'

'Nuala, when are you going to stop it? You can see she is restless.'

'Stop it? For what? She's smiling all over her face, so she is. I'll get you another cup of tea.'

'There's fight in the people of Ulster,' said another of the judges who came to tea and to see Margaret's garden. 'They will not make concessions to the enemy, now, or ever.' If there was anything ambivalent about the word 'enemy' we didn't raise it.

We went into the dining-room to see one of the large Irish linen cloths on the table, and the judge's eyes were around the room taking in the porcelain and the quality of the silver. By the end of that holiday we had learnt, in the present circumstances, the sheer art of talking without really saying anything at all.

'If it's jokes that keeps you going that's OK by me,' said you, lighting a cigarette and forgetting about the one burning in the ashtray.

We then had one of your medical student jokes which exploded the tea party in two, the judge grinning and Margaret and Gerald wondering when the story was to reach its point.

But as Michael and I discovered when we were in Kenya the British take their afternoon tea, their cricket, their talent for queuing, their plum puddings, wherever they go, because, at all costs, the show must go on. With Margaret and Gerald 'the show' was an observance of the niceties of life, coupled with the Picto-Celt overriding sense of hospitality.

It has to be said that the Anglo-Saxon-style Christmas on the Equator is perhaps one of endurance. At both a temperature and a humidity soaring into the 90s, the turkey assumes a sort of defiance in the process of being stuffed, and those round the table, chattering about the pleasure of bread sauce and cranberry jelly, cast an admiring eye at a fellow creature that has been in the precincts of hell. We had been invited by the General and his family, and before leaving home we warned Simon not to say lucky buggers to everything the General's pretty little daughters said. Mind you, Peggy, the sweet pretty little daughters travelled in the same army truck to school – the soldiers with their guns facing outwards at the ready – and had their vocabulary increased by the sons and daughters of the Kenya settlers.

On this occasion the only bird the General was watching was on the table, and, with the skill peculiar to surgeons, butchers and soldiers, began to carve.

My love of the African interior *was* passed on to you and Peter. You went there twice, and the photographs told the story of your conversion.

In the African bush one whispers. It's the fear that a sudden movement or noise might upset the pattern of life that is several million years older than yourself. Africans know about it. Did you ever see the lolloping walk/run of the Masai when he has far to go? At the end of the journey there may be a change of red murram cloak, dyed by their red mud, and a meal of home-made curd, consisting of blood, yoghurt and urine, all taken from the cows.

You've got two cats at home, Peggy, not from Kenya but from Egypt, their long slanting eyes have been seen on vases, in frescoes, decorating the inside walls of pyramids. I wonder if it's ownership of these Nubian cats that found you the ancient necklace you brought back from Egypt.

The cat that is attached to this nursing home remains attached, in spite of illness and death, because it senses, as do the patients, that love and understanding is here.

We leave your bedroom door open all the time now. But you're not looking out, you're hardly opening your eyes. You're somewhere though, because every now and again in a big voice you say a word, and the noise, and the surprise of it, wakes you: 'Where did that come from?' you say.

Where indeed, with the little strength remaining.

Michael, who was so neutralized in Africa, and receptive, did not get so much from Ulster as we'd hoped. Mind you, he was well matched in charm there. If anyone kept his charm polished it was Michael. As I've said, Bessie had a soft spot for him. Besides, she liked men. To her, Father was God's second representative here on earth; Mike was, shall we say, the beloved John of the Gospel; and Michael was a visiting centurion – not, I am sure, guilty of anything at Calvary. Michael attended weddings with us in Mourne, tried hard to be equally nice to all forty cousins, and confirmed the idea of some of the men of Ulster that the English are a stuck-up, patronizing bunch. They knew about his massive chestful of decorations, and could forgive a lot. But the truth of the matter is that he is not an Ulsterman.

Richard, on the other hand, who had come over from France at the time of William the Conqueror, and with his surname Neville, had an entrance to both countries, and found the Irish (to him all the same) moving at about the pace he liked, living the way he liked, and could down a jar of whiskey like the best of them. I tried a follow-up by introducing him to some of the Irish writers, but the point about Richard was that he had a highly advanced mathematical brain, and had not got the imagination for poetry and novels because he could not *see* the places described. Dialogue in books he could handle, but he still felt that writers should have an in-built editor at work in their heads; the same, let us say, for conversation outside books. Richard spoke when he had something to say. He did not go in for chatter.

'What d'ye do for a living?' he'd be asked in Ulster, and Richard who'd had 'a good war' said: 'I don't.'

'Good man,' was their retort, 'work never did anyone any good.'

I suppose I'd be rich today if Richard hadn't more or less drunk and gambled away his capital.

Why should a nice, relaxed, unambitious, gentle man like him take to drink? I'll tell you.

His father pushed off, leaving Richard with his sister and mother in a fairly impecunious state, when Richard was fourteen. Mind you, having visited Richard's mother a time or two, I could see why the poor man went to Alaska. He complicated matters making a bigamous marriage, and sending home his bastard to find out if there were any spoils after all the great-uncles had died. Richard's father, Ralph, died ten days before the big inheritance came, so Richard got the lot. But, before that, his mother had married again, someone commanding the Guards

Depot at Windsor, and he, the colonel, insisted on formal dinner each night, with Richard aged sixteen staying behind with the port. Early in his relationship with his stepfather he found that drink loosened his tongue. But that by no means was all of it, because he was the victim of one of those pernicious genes, handed down from both father and mother, that fed off alcohol.

On one of my last visits to Richard's mother, I was startled by the sudden opening of her eyes — piercing blue like her son's. She was by then perpetually in a nursing home with a beaker of whisky by her bed — this was no drying-out home. In her frail voice she said: 'What is *really* the matter with Richard?' Of course, I didn't tell her, but I think my moment of hesitation probably confirmed her belief.

There's been a belief that drunks are what they are through feelings of inadequacy. Richard did not have feelings of inadequacy. He was an alcoholic, and alcoholics are set on a downward course with the first taste of alcohol. And it's a very painful business to watch the struggle against the inevitable.

It's quite early on Sunday morning, Peggy, and I've come through streets where houses and people in them are deep in sleep. There is altogether quiet.

During the short intense latter stage of your illness it's been difficult for my mind to be anywhere else but in this little room. Except, of course, when we've extended it to bring the past into the present. Outside events have been diminished to the size of the television screen. So now let's give you a peep into some of these houses as they come awake:

It'll be croissants and real coffee in the better-off families, probably in bed, the tray brought up by the husband who familiarizes himself with the kitchen on Sundays. Possibly further down the social scale there will be a variety of cereals, including muesli, out on the kitchen table, for everyone to help themselves. In my household there are also raisins in a little bowl – for those over fifty – and in Simon's house on a Sunday morning, there will be porridge, made by Simon, and free-range eggs, boiled by Simon. This is his day, and this is his favourite meal. He'll pore over the *Sunday Times* – looking at the sports page first, to see if the Chelsea football team, even in summer, is being discussed. And then it will be the centre pages for the news. His twelve-year-old son, Nicholas, called after his uncle, is now in competition for the sports page. Nick, on the other hand, will have been up early, taking his son James for his rugby coaching. At one point Nick coached the team in which James played, and it so happens that the team won at Twickenham. Proud? I'll say. Your John will be in the big double bed with Alicia and between them, sitting upright, bright and alert, is Julia, welcoming in the morning.

I know by the way you are moving, Peggy, that you're in pain. It comes in sharp stabs, and I'm not sure you know exactly from where. There have been moments when pain is all you are. But the doctors have found the right medicine for you now. The nursing home had said it may be impossible to increase the dose. What are they afraid of? Administering a fatal dose? No. They are concerned that you should not be sick. The feeling of nausea is possibly worse than the feeling of pain. They do not want either the discomfort, nor the indignity for you. Now I understand that *you* have understood that what is happening is the taking over from your very considerable will.

It's difficult for you. The nursing staff, from the matron down, are impressed by your determination not to betray the profession to which you belong by a display of letting go. But the truth is that letting go might, in a sense, be its own release. Play it your way, Peggy, your own very courageous way.

Talking of bladders, which we were, but only indirectly, do you remember how when we were first in London, and I was taken short outside the Ritz, you said: 'Come on.' So, bold as brass, we strode into this famous West End hotel and tried to look as if we were staying there, and that we knew exactly where the ladies' room was. Down the stairs we went, you first, and sailed into this room of lovely lit glass and plush seats. We emerged from the Ritz to find that we had developed a taste for high living, and proceeded to visit the Berkeley, then the Park Lane and the Piccadilly. It says much for the interior designers that the loos were all different, because, after all, a hole in the ground is a hole in the ground, no matter what's on top.

Mind you, when we did encounter merely the hole

in the ground in a public lavatory in the gardens of the Topkapi Museum in Istanbul, we wished a thousand flights back to the Ritz. *There* were these figures swathed in black, crouched like mother hens on a nest, talking chattily to each other. There were places for the feet, and nothing else. I stood frozen, and you, standing well back on your heels and your chin up, said: 'Come on.' Our bare arms, trousers, sun tops, sun tan, were hideously conspicuous in this dungeon of a place.

I'll get off the subject of loos, Peggy, because, if you remember, Uncle James would have none of it. When Mike came home from school one holiday with a particularly dirty schoolboy lavatory joke and gave it to us at lunch, Uncle James sent him to his room for the day. I've since wondered if it was the biblical attitude to sodomy that influenced my father to this degree about anything to do with bottoms. Mild sex jokes he could handle. Aunt Marj on the other hand couldn't really handle either, so developed a smile which became a shy giggle when she thought someone was reaching the end of the story and she might not like it.

It was unusual for Mike to hold the floor, because we had a professional story-teller in our family — understandable enough when you think that clergymen spend their time talking to a room of silence. But it might, it just might, have been the prospect of a rival that sent Mike to his room for the whole of that day. Preaching is a strange phenomenon in that it gets passive acceptance. Quaker meetings might have done a thing or two to show congregation participation, particularly to the Presbyterian church. I used to wonder if God had a book of recorded sermons, with little boxes at the foot of each page, saying: very acceptable, acceptable, possible, and untenable.

Our journey through the smart hotels, was, of course, our desire to be part of the good life, because at the time we had meagre salaries, you working in a clinic and I in the War Office. From my father in terms of allowance came £10 a month. I shared a one-bedroomed flat with an old school friend, and the only way we could pay the rent was for me to model – but unknown to the Manse of Crossmichael. One unhappy day a village housewife bought a knitting pattern in Castle Douglas, and there on the front of it was the minister's daughter modelling a bed-jacket over a flimsy night-dress. A missive wired its way to Ebury Street here in London, and I was home in Scotland for a time.

The hotel I have not mentioned in my remembering is the Dorchester. We sailed in there with heads high, acknowledging the nod from the doorman because we had been there a time or two before, visiting our very rich relation, Cousin Flora from Canada. On one occasion she invited us to lunch to meet the last surviving daughter of Queen Victoria, Princess Alice. Her husband, the Earl of Athlone, had been Governor-General of Canada, and whilst there they had been entertained by Cousin Flora in her French château, brought stone by stone from

France at the time when she was feeling European and was also negotiating a palazzo in Venice.

She came each year to the Chelsea Flower Show, bringing over her Rolls, chauffeur and one gardener, and whilst here, using one of her relations to play lady's maid. My only taxi ride with her taught me a thing or two about the very rich: they never carry money. The interior of her bag would be like the Queen's: powder compact, lipstick, linen handkerchief, and possibly a list of the names of the people she was going to meet.

The luncheon for Princess Alice was given in the Oliver Messel Suite at the top of the hotel. To say it was sumptuous is to insult the designer. To say it was artistic, in a garden floral way, does not yet match the beauty of the climbing roses on the walls. The round table in this round room made the process of building up conversation easier, though one has to admit that a first close encounter with Royalty is stupidly nerve-racking. You and I, Peggy, were brought in to chat up the luncheon guests. I was supposed to be an asset – I wrote books, and you were brought in because Cousin Flora thought it was clever of you – pretty little thing that you were – to be a practising doctor, and she enjoyed introducing you as Dr Fry to see the look of surprise on the guests' faces.

'You a doctor! My, my, you do surprise me.'

Fools, couldn't they see the brains bursting out of your face?

The House of Windsor skin had been handed

down to Princess Alice. Hers was of a pink pearl quality, and as I spent a great deal of time studying the face for itself, it was rather lost on me that we were in touch with a large piece of history. We had touched this ninety-year-old lady who had touched those who had touched those who lived in the century before last.

Claudette, the black nurse who likes to stand in the door and look has moved in cautiously to ask: 'How could He let this happen to someone who has done so much good?' But that question would not be from Nuala. Nuala knows. Nuala knows that God can be as irrational as those made in His image. She says it's no good saying: 'It's bound to rain tomorrow because it's my day off.' Justice, she has learnt, is something invented by man because everything has to make sense in his terms.

The nurse, who's still standing here, asks if I'd like some tea. 'No thank you,' I say, because the other black nurse has just given me coffee. It's a feature of this nursing home that families of the patients are cherished. But you, in a surprisingly loud voice, say: 'I'd like some.'

So they've come back with tea in a pot, one cup and saucer, a jog of milk and one feeding cup.

'Where's the sugar?' say you with your eyes shut. So the tea will be poured carefully into the feeding cup, because that big voice means you are not, for the time being, to be the invalid. Invalid, Peggy, is such an inadequate word for what you are going through. But I will help you drink from the feeding cup, because in the action of doing it we have a second of normality. And you say to me in a soft voice: 'When is Robert coming?'

Soon, Peggy, there will be only Peter, John and myself to come and see you, because we sense that you can't now handle others. Your lifelong friend, Joan, has gone back to Australia, because her return ticket was up, and staying with Peter for three weeks put a strain on her. But we know that a part of her is staying behind.

I have already been sent out of the room by you, once when we were quite young, and again the other day.

The incident when young was that I was sent to Coventry for telling on you and Mike baring your parts again, for not letting me in on the game. Later I had the idea that around the middle teens you and Mike quite fancied each other. Actually I don't think you did, looking back on it now, but you had something even better: you could indulge in emotion, feeling, and, given the chance, experimentation.

I wasn't exactly sent out of the room the other day, I was just told to go away.

I had come in to find you, miraculously sitting cross-legged on the floor, a little Buddha, and, fearing that you'd catch cold or harm yourself (one goes on with it), I tried to lift you up onto the bed. I got the command: 'Stop!' And then: 'You can go.' Imperious would you say?

I sat in the hall, my thoughts for once going out

of the nursing home and onto the subject of the Republican Movement, and how I'd retained a lingering sympathy for it: remember that the good jobs, houses, favoured positions went always to the Protestant. But now that the IRA don't necessarily represent all of Catholic Ulster, and have descended to intermittent butchery, my feelings are against them. Their targets have been democracy, political solutions, judges, lawyers, policemen, soldiers, men, women and children. As I left the hall into my mind came some of the vile acts of the Loyalist gangs and I said out into the passageway: 'Let's hope the community will isolate them all.'

This time you stretched your thin arm, and trying to lift my hand, you bent as if to kiss it.

You are silent, and very still now. I hope that was not the last piece of action from you.

We've had discussions in the past, you and I, about the Troubles. I've said that a good therapist should show compassion to all mankind, with its problems.

'You can't show compassion to a psychopath who's sitting there wondering when he can do you.'

'Are you sure?' said I, testing you.

'It'll be a great day when psychiatry has understood the mind of the psychopath.'

'But analysis should...'

'Should? I'll tell you this: psychiatry reckons to appeal to the reasonable instinct in man...'

'The two don't go together.'

'...and with most patients it's there. Not so your

psychopath. He knows the difference between right and wrong, but doesn't care.'

'If your profession has understood that far, they could go a step further.'

'Cousin dear, there's a kick in killing, and very few killers want to be reasoned out of it. Anyway...'

'Anyway?'

'Drop the bone. You've been worrying at it long enough.'

They're going away now, my liberal views. It was the history teacher at school who taught me to look at both sides in every situation. It was even good for passing exams because you tended to have double the facts, as well as double the theories. Her hero was Winston Churchill, because he had the courage to cross the floor of the House of Commons, not once, but twice. Rigid minds she could not tolerate.

'In my profession,' you have said, 'you have to appear confident and certain otherwise the patient will turn dialogue round to question *you*.'

'Ah!'

Do you hear anything on the radio now, Peggy? I mean – do you take anything in? I came in two days ago to hear you say: 'It's finished.' As the radio was still droning away, I wondered if you were talking about hope, your life, or even possibly of Jesus on the cross. You've been even quieter since, and you may be at some distant spot, so I'll conjure up more pictures to see if you want to come back.

How about when you and Peter drove down to

Berkshire to Nick's wedding? It was at the in-law's house. The sun shone, brilliantly, many guests arrived, filling the house and the garden, and Clare's father made a speech about being denied a walk down the aisle with his daughter. If you remember, Nick and Clare already had one-year-old, white-blond James, and Clare was pregnant with another. On the morning that Nick was to be married, and when driving to Berkshire with me, he said: 'My God! I haven't bought a wedding ring.' As wedding rings on the M4 are not easy to find I debated taking off the one Richard had given me – knowing he'd loved Nick and wouldn't mind. But we made a detour or two, bought the ring, and proceeded on our way.

Only parents and brothers were invited to the registry office; the rest of the families and friends met up afterwards. That's what I mean when I say the house bulged – all the relations on our side.

The day went well. Strangers to Clare had no idea she was pregnant. Her best friend, who is a dress designer, made a camouflaging dress of such beauty and skill that Clare did not look at all out of proportion. She looked radiant. You, Peggy, electric ever, and full of the good wine, with your high, high-heeled shoes sinking into the slightly damp grass, saying to my second sister-in-law, Sita, whose name is the Indian word for peace: 'Shita, I'm shinking!'

You looked like a wood elf on stilts, in a silk dress that seemed to match the garden. Cousin Midge Burridge of Desert Orchid fame was wearing one of the only two hats at the wedding. Mine was the other. Both were red, mine a straw boater borrowed from a friend, who had borrowed it from a friend, and Midge's was felt, wide-brimmed, with the largest white feather any of us had seen.

The best adult photograph ever taken of you was at Nick's and Clare's wedding. You are laughing fit to burst, mouth stretched from ear to ear, and even Peter was smiling that day. I have the photograph, already framed. There were only a few of us who knew you had already been told you had cancer.

The only time I felt murderous about Peter was once when we were already – before leaving the house – late. We crawled down the road to Heathrow at about twenty miles per hour, with Peter telling us not to flap. *He* wasn't risking his life in a piece of metal taking to the air to go to one of the worst trouble areas in the world.

It's a bit of a shock the first time you go to Terminal One, to find that you, who are travelling to Northern Ireland, are sharing a departure lounge with those going to other trouble spots, and both of you a mile on mile walk away from the other departure lounges.

Last year I took you around in a wheelchair, and I had to tell you to stop smoking and telling jokes.

It was the same when we went to Madeira. Once we'd got you into the wheelchair we piled the luggage on top of you, and an official or two approached to say that it would be doing the patient no good.

'There's no patients here,' said you, and the official smiling and looking as if he'd swop place with you any day.

You were happy that day at the wedding, the sun shining out of your eyes, and your reassurances to the mainly English guests: 'We don't all come from the Falls Road.'

'Oh really! Oh really!' as if they couldn't see you were joking. I've noticed it before when talking to 'foreigners' – they have a hazy idea of the contours of Ireland, but they *know* that Belfast occupies most of the north, the six counties somehow squeezed in under it.

Each year returning from Killowen we travel the M1 (theirs), and each year we manage to miss the turning for the airport, and are into West Belfast, and the sign ahead is the FALLS ROAD.

'We'd better get out of here before anyone asks a question.'

'If anyone asks a question, you shut up. I'll answer.' And you could too, the best Belfast dock accent, cultivated by your brother Paul and taken with him to Scotland.

Last year we were talking so hard we did it again, with me driving and you making play with a map, turning it upside down and twisting your neck.

'For God's sake, we're in it again.'

'Now what?'

'Let's make a U-turn and go back to where we went wrong.'

'And where was that?'

'Go on – turn.'

'Don't be daft, there are police everywhere.'

'They're not looking for us.'

'How would *you* know? You with your English accent, fair hair and pink skin.'

'It's not pink. I've got quite a tan.'

And so on. You loving every moment of it. We escaped the entanglements of city life, back onto the M1, and did not talk again until we hit the airport.

We returned the hired car to a little garage near the airport that didn't look as if it belonged to anything, least of all to Hertz.

'So you're there,' said the man in the garage, as if he'd been waiting for us all morning. 'I see you've got a full tank. Good girls. How did it go?'

'Just fine. I think I'll exchange my car for a Vauxhall,' said I, full of the refresher course on charm.

'Sure yous wouldn't regret it. It would take you anywhere, so it would.'

It had. Backwards and forwards over the border, you looking to see if any of your mother's tired, doped cows were on their way up or down.

'Did you go inland at all? County Tyrone is great. There are some grand houses there,' said he looking at me, and you muttering: 'I told you!'

We went to one of the grand houses in Tyrone, turning in at some fine gates and starting a climb up the longest drive I've ever been on, and half-way up forgetting we were on a drive, and saying to Margaret what a beautiful county Tyrone was.

'We're still on Fiona's drive,' said Margaret, caressing with fond looks the huge trees around us.

We had a lunch of farmyard chicken, vegetables from the garden, and the Irish potato. Oh what an ode I could write. This was followed by raspberries and cream – the cream from the local farm and the raspberries from the garden.

We ate in the dining-room at garden level, a magnificent bay window showing us the gardens, the trees, and Tyrone beyond. Her two dogs, large and small – and looking like the painting *Dignity and Impudence* – lay under the sideboard, each with one eye open in case there was a move to go out, or the chance of a piece of dropped chicken. One of them was fuzz and wool from top to bottom, and you said, 'That dog looks as if its mother mated with a rug.'

I've heard that the half-rug has died, so the next time we . . . I go there, there may be another one.

We drove home through Tyrone, Armagh, and finally back to Down. Apart from the Falls and Shankhill Road, and the Bogside in Derry, Down and Armagh have the most of the IRA 'incidents'. Euphemisms should have no place in Ulster, but perhaps it's a language adopted for those who have to live in the bad areas. I'll spell it out: the 'trouble spots' are the border of Armagh with Eire, the area around Newry, half in and half out of Ulster. Rostrevor occasionally getting a backlash, otherwise it is a beautiful extending village nestling at the foot of the Mourne Mountains – as the travel guides would say. Rostrevor runs in to Warrenpoint at one end, and at the other into the housing estate where some of 'the bad boys' hang out.

The point about the 'B Special' is that he knew every man in the district, and precisely what they were doing at any given moment. They were brutal, say the Catholic population, and tough on our 'wee boys'.

Of course they were tough, every organization has its tough members. It wasn't for nothing that I had this time as the commanding officer's wife of one of the Para battalions. Tough? You should have seen and heard them. The miracle to me is that in Northern Ireland those in the SAS and the Paras and several other units haven't caused more in the way of secular killing. To be provoked and provoked by boys hurling stones and rocks when you're under orders not to shoot, dressed in heavy khaki drill, hot, furious, and on the point of letting go, must be the severest of tests.

Of course *you* have no sympathy with these people, or their cause, and as a doctor you've had to pick up the pieces of human being from time to time. It maddens you that other countries ship arms to the IRA, holding in their hearts some romantic notion of the starving Irish peasant. Murderous thoughts are what we all have when we've been witness to any of the bomb outrages. Mind you, if thought could kill, then many of us are guilty. I've wished Michael dead a time or two, but with a certain magnanimity. I saw him as the hero in the Middle East when he and his battalion were guarding King Hussein, and allowing him a noble death. In Kenya, on one occasion, I wished him into the jaws of a crocodile when we were pushing a Land Rover across a river. There was nothing noble in my thinking then. I wanted him crunched and swallowed.

You, Peggy, would have put John's stepmother into boiling oil several times over. But the trouble about murderous thinking is that you can't always project it out of yourself. Mine, as you know, went inwards for quite a number of years, and evil's accomplice at times can be the body. It rebels under the weight of all that ferocious thinking, and throws up ulcers, muscle spasms, chronic sinusitus, and, yes, one must say it, cancer. But you know all that. You're not taking your cancer out on anyone now except perhaps your mother who handed down that gene which had killed her – and with it a whole lot of negative thinking about motherhood.

Get rid of the ego, say three-quarters of the world, while the remaining Christian quarter talks about free will.

Ask Tolstoy how many times he thought about getting rid of the self when he was slotting the six sides of himself into the six main characters in *War and Peace*. Ask Balzac if the million grains of coffee he consumed each morning helped in the disbanding of the I Am. And consider if the world had never seen the last great, great self-portraits by Rembrandt.

But . . . is the little bird that has landed on the slim branch of the climbing rose outside this window any less great? And, what is it balancing with? One day the man creature will just step off into space and go. Man will fly, but, of course, it won't be called flying.

Can you hear me, Peggy? Peter tells me that he's looked in the place you said you had hidden your Egyptian necklace, but there's nothing there. He is wondering if you ever had it. You had it, all right, I even put it round my neck to convince myself of its reality, beautiful mysterious object that it is. And now I'm wondering – because it's strange, isn't it, that we are the only two to have seen it since 4,000 BC? – if the Colonel was right when he talked about my other incarnations. He would have known about you.

You have opened an eye. Something has told you that your cousin is sitting here. I wonder what you thought of my novels, particularly *The Cousins*, that was about the four cousins. You didn't say much about it. Relations don't. They never see themselves, or anyone else for that matter, as the author sees them. They're always the nice person who lives next door, and never the actual target. I think I did you well in that novel, making you into a dark-eyed chip off the old block of Ireland. I even indicated feyness, and got away with it.

I'd really like to read you *Ulysses*, and let the words wash over you; the sheer flowing poetry of it, and the misty Dublin voices.

You've produced one of your 'no's, Peggy, and I think it is about the book. It's not that you don't rate it; I think you're telling me that it would be all wrong to hear me read it. You're right, of course.

And I never did like the sound of my father reading Burns.

I don't think I ever realized that your eyes are exactly the same as mine. I received quite a shock just now when you opened both and actually looked *at* me. It was almost as if at the same moment we had the same thought. They are Fisher eyes: big, grey-green with a touch of the sea thrown in – on stormy days. I've handed mine on to Simon – if you see what I mean. It's really only about the eyes that he's like me. He's very much his own person, long, willowy; he should be in nineteenth-century dress. My women friends all slightly fancy him. What they don't know is that he isn't the slightest bit interested in reading novels or poetry, or playing the piano, and *is* interested in football, pulling things to pieces to see how they work, and having baby sons with his lovely wife Miranda. But what he hasn't got is your John's voice. John's voice is both soft and seductive, the sort of voice that should be at a bedside, or, better still, in bed with you.

I think John will remain close to me. We'll console each other, and almost certainly the talking will go on. I mean mine to you. I can't imagine a world without the familiar banter.

The room is getting darker, shadows shortening, the nursing home staff going about with soft feet, and Nuala looks in to give a smile and a light touch to your shoulder. Her ballad singing is over, she has sensed the moment for it to stop, and now she sits quietly by my side. We have said you do not want a visit from the vicar of St Mary's Church because you cannot imagine what words he could find that would alter your condition – kind, understanding man that he is. The departure is something you're managing on your own. The struggle to get out of bed, the restlessness with your arms – almost as if you were swimming away – has ceased, because at last you have dismissed the part of you that is holding you back. There's a little curve of a smile on your face, and the last of the wrinkles disappearing, almost as if they'd never been.

The silent composed beauty of you is something new, perhaps a little frightening – have you already gone? I must quickly sum up some of the conclusions we have reached, *you* have reached, in case I have got it wrong, misunderstood. I *think* we have understood, in our own way, that the essentially material and the essentially aesthetic can combine because one is nothing without the other; yet, strangely, the aesthetic comes about as a need to be shot of the *function* of the body, which ultimately must be seen as a freedom that would have no meaning had there not first been the prison. A coin does not exist unless it has two sides – the eternal union, the no escape, the long, long acceptance.

'Long,' you say as you settle into your chair. It is the chair for the dying, the chair of support, the chair in which you are given freedom.

But first I must tell you, Peggy, in case you think it was a dream, that moonlight came into your room last night, and with it came Robert. Nuala, attendant on her patient, and understanding the situation, let him in through the front door. They crept down the corridor almost as if some of your history might bar the way to him, but Nuala hissing: 'It's about time. What kept you?' And he coming into the room with the white flowers that are beside you now, and you knowing he was there, and you both believing in what was happening, and he watching you fall into a long, very long, sleep.

POSTSCRIPT

W<small>E</small> <small>TOOK</small> <small>YOUR</small> <small>ASHES</small> to Northern Ireland, Peggy, and put them in with the relations. John couldn't accept your idea of scattering them in the mountains towards the little fields. He wanted a focus, somewhere we could come to, put down flowers and remember – though we all know that remembering is already a part of each day. So, the present minister of the Mourne church in Kilkeel donned all his robes one fine summer's day in the middle of the week, and spoke nice-sounding words over the grave. We had, of course, for Peter's sake, already had a cremation service in London.

John brought over the casket – precious load that it is – but I knew you were only half in it. When we started to put the casket into the grave of Senator Joe Fisher – a lovely man whose filing system was always in the outside pockets of his bulging jacket – we found it was too full. We moved you a little to the right – you were ever that, Peggy – and there was the imposing headstone of our grandparents, with room in front.

'This is it,' I said. 'She'll be with her Grannie.'

The casket was lowered into the soil, and from somewhere a distant voice said: 'I'll come back from time to time to visit it.'

I'm not sure if the smile on my face was fully understood, but then not many knew that I had already booked myself in there for when my turn comes.

When Memory Dies
A. Sivanandan

A three-generational saga of a Sri Lankan family's search for coherence and continuity in a country broken by colonial occupation and riven by ethnic wars. *Winner of the Sagittarius Prize 1998* and *shortlisted for the Commonwealth Writers Prize 1998*

'Haunting ... with an immense tenderness. The extraordinary poetic tact of this book makes it unforgettable' – John Berger, *Guardian*

The Last Kabbalist of Lisbon
Richard Zimler

A literary mystery set among secret Jews living in Lisbon in 1506 when, during Passover celebrations, some two thousand Jewish inhabitants were murdered in a pogrom. THE INTERNATIONAL BESTSELLER.

'Remarkable erudition and compelling imagination, an American Umberto Eco' – Francis King, *Spectator*

Night Letters
Robert Dessaix

Every night for twenty nights in a hotel room in Venice, a man recently diagnosed with HIV writes a letter home to a friend. He describes not only the kaleidoscopic journey he has just made from Switzerland across northern Italy to Venice, but reflects on questions of mortality, seduction and the search for paradise.

'Dessaix writes with great elegance, with passion, compassion, and sly wit. Literally a wonderful book' – John Banville

Isabelle
John Berger and Nella Bielski

A compelling recreation of the life of Isabelle Eberhardt.

'A tantalizing enigma, Berger and Bielski's filmic approach is appropriate to her literally dramatic life, and the symmetry of the imagery is an indication of the artistry of this work' – *Observer*